THE SMALLEST
VILLAGE

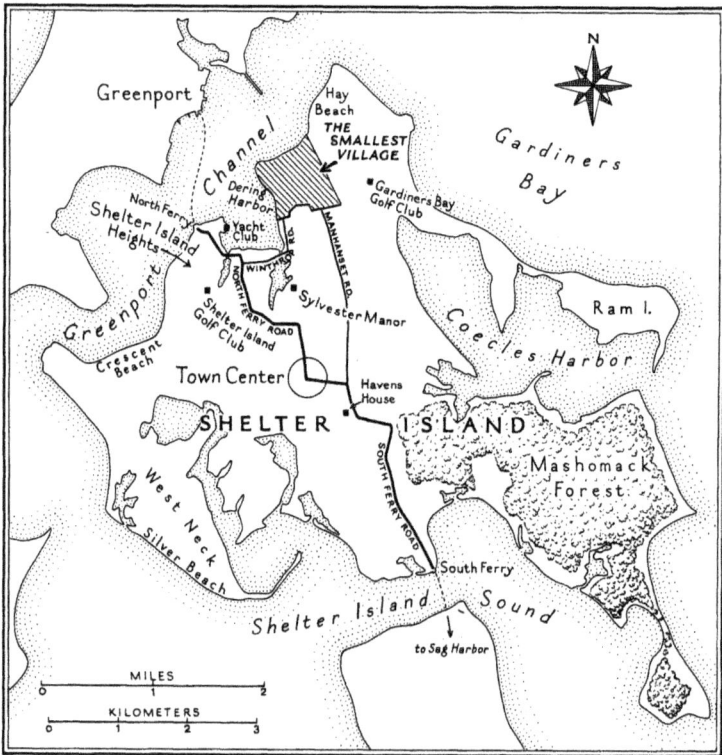

Skeleton Map of Shelter Island drawn by George Colbert, based on sketch plan prepared by Susan Gustafson

THE SMALLEST VILLAGE

The Story of Dering Harbor
Shelter Island, New York
1874-1974

Stewart W. Herman

Brick Tower Press
Manhanset House

Brick Tower Press
New York

Brick Tower Press
Manhanset House
Dering Harbor, New York 11965-0342
bricktower@aol.com

www.BrickTowerPress.com

The Brick Tower Press colophon is a registered trademark of J. T Colby & Company, Inc.

Second Edition
Library of Congress Cataloging in Publication Data
Herman, Stewart Winfield, 1909-2006
The smallest village.
Includes index.
1. Dering Harbor, Shelter Island, N. Y.—History. I. Title.
F129.D377H47   974.7'25   76-51
ISBN 978-1-899694-61-7

The title page illustration is a contemporary woodcut of the first Manhanset House

Table of Contents

SITES OF FORMER STRUCTURES

a. Manhanset House
b. Chapel
c. Hotel Stables & Water Tower
d. Old Village Hall
e. Hotel Annex
f. Benjamin Atha
g. Tarrant Putnam
h. New York Yacht Club
i. Firt Poor Cottage
j. A. Schwarzmann
k. Lidgerwood
l. Carl Pickhardt
m. Firehouse & Superintendent's Cottage
n. Hotel Dock

EXISTING STRUCTURES
(as of 1976)

1. Village Hall
2. Ian Brownlie
3. Baylis-Brownlie
4. Stewart Herman
5. Mathias Komor
6. Vernon O'Rourke
7. George Read
8. Walter Glaws
9. May Edwards
10. James Blackburn
11. Harold Weaver
12. George Genung
13. William Allan
14. Arnott White
15. Thomas Wilcox
16. Henrietta Roig
17. Morgan Ames
18. Samuel Hird
19. Peter Holnback
20. Bridgford Hunt
21. Jane Kohl
22. Peacock-Adams
23. Arthur Roth
24. Rachel Carpenter
25. Florence McCormick
26. Clifton Phalen
27. Stanley Giannelli
28. John Reeve
29. Carl Gustafson
30. Harvey Woolhiser
31. Tone Kwas
32. Florence Hench
33. Maintenance Area & Water Tower

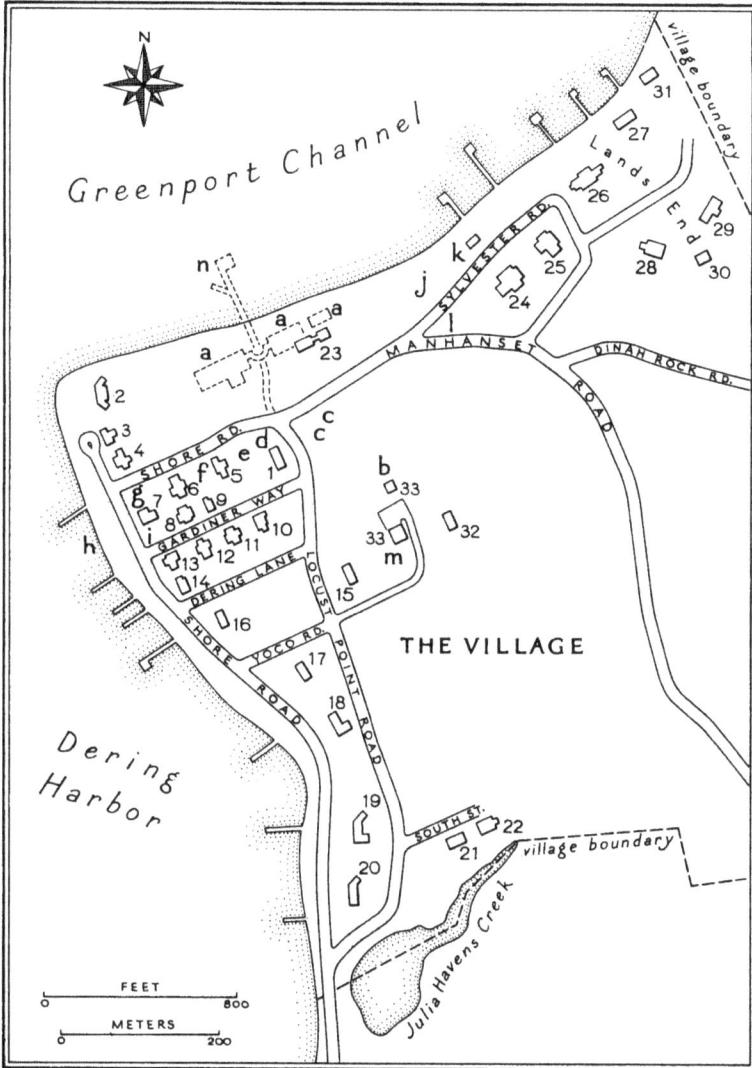

N

Greenport Channel

village boundary

31
27
Lands End
26
29
28 30

n
a a
a
23
24
25
j k
SYLVESTER RD.
MANHANSET ROAD
DINAH ROCK RD.

2
3
4
SHORE RD.
f e d
5 6 c c
7
b
33
32
g 7
8 9
i GARDINER WAY
10
33
m
11
12
13
14
DERING LANE
h
15
16
SHORE ROAD
YOCO RD.
LOCUST POINT ROAD
THE VILLAGE

17
18

19

Dering Harbor

20

SOUTH ST.
21 22
village boundary

Julia Havens Creek

FEET
0   800
METERS
0   200

Map drawn by George Colbert, based on sketch plan
prepared by Susan Gustafson

Period post card that guests could send from the Manhanset House Post Office

THE AUTHOR is indebted—and very grateful—to the host of individuals who answered his endless questions, and to his wife who typed and retyped so many of these pages. He is duly appreciative of the honor of being appointed Village historian, without which impulse the book would not have been written. Special thanks are due to the *Suffolk Weekly Times* for repeated access to old files which, for lack of other records, proved to be a uniquely valuable resource.

The author is grateful to Susan Gustafson for preparing the drawings that illustrate the book.

Finally, the author wishes to thank the Shelter Island Historical Society for generously taking this project under its wing. Its solicitation of pre-publication subscriptions, and—not least—the outright donations of Florence McCormick, Clifton Phalen, Henrietta Roig, Arthur Roth and Thomas Wilcox have helped to make this limited edition possible.

Hotel's Bathing Beach on Dering Harbor with pavilion for tea and music

Chapter 1

A BIT OF BACKGROUND

THE VILLAGE of Dering Harbor has frequently been called the smallest incorporated village in New York State, perhaps in the whole country. No sustained effort has been made to determine whether this is really so, but there would appear to be some truth in the assertion.

The facts are that it comprises a mere two hundred acres, no more than a good-sized farm, and exactly thirty households, only four of which are inhabited the year round. Mayor Ian Brownlie, a conscientious weekender, speaks of his bailiwick as "the smallest political unit in the United States" and has not, so far, been contradicted. Ghost towns of smaller dimensions and zero populations may perhaps be found in the once-golden west but Dering Harbor is decisively not *that* sort of community. Skeletons in closets, maybe; ghosts not yet!

The Village is legally incorporated and conducts its own affairs in a Colonial-style hall flanked by a sixty-foot flagpole. The duly elected mayor, the clerk and the Board of Trustees meet for about three hours once a month, on a Saturday morning unless otherwise arranged. The affairs themselves encompass such municipal business as an independent water supply system, trash collection, and general maintenance of roads and grounds, plus a dash of other matters pertaining to the welfare and improvement of a predominantly summertime residency. Taxes are collected, of course. The annual budget runs to about $35,000.

Too often the terms "village" and "town" are used indiscriminately, but not in this story. The *Village* of Dering Harbor is part—in fact, one fortieth part—of the *Town* of Shelter Island, whose boundaries happen to be identical with those of the Island itself. As the Town is older than the Village and the Island is much older than the Town, some preliminary remarks about each may be in order.

The island is a moderately large mouthful of land strategically lodged between the crocodilian jaws of eastern Long Island. With the aid of a map and a modicum of fantasy, one can easily imagine this morsel of 8,000 appetizing acres being washed by Peconic waters right down the Empire State's thirsty throat. Fortunately, a severe case of geologic lockjaw intervened centuries ago to prevent Orient Point from clamping down on Montauk.

That saved Shelter Island. Since then it swims serenely within the larger island's protective jaws—whence the name *Ahaquatawamok*, "island-sheltered-by-islands". By nature this bite of land, roughly four miles by seven, constitutes a peaceful place, abundantly endowed with wooded hills, fresh ponds, quiet creeks and pleasant beaches. Rough waves and high winds are by no means unknown, but as a rule their full force expends itself in getting here, not unlike the tired glaciers which deposited a few spent boulders on these shores ten thousand years ago.

Politically the island is a township, one of ten in the largely rural County of Suffolk. It is rock-ribbed Republican by about three to one, and fiercely protective of all public and private prerogatives. As one well-known newspaperman and summer resident, Harold C. Schonberg, aptly expressed it, the Islanders "loudly extol the virtues of private enterprise, local rights and religion."[1] This essentially Yankee population, small at best, rises and falls with tidal regularity. In winter it now numbers about 1,900 souls but between May and September the trundling ferries inflate that figure by a few thousand seasonal residents and some transients.

Except for some very soothing scenery, the attraction for sightseers is minimal. The typical tourist is about as infrequent as an authentic harelegger. Membership in this species is quite special. The exact meaning of the term harelegger is in dispute. But by those who do claim it, the sobriquet is worn with considerable pride. Only a person actually born on the Island—not in the hospital across the channel!—is entitled to bear it. Having been born here, he (or she) carries it with him (or her) whenever and wherever he (or she) moves.

According to the most commonly accepted explanation, the name was once originally (and somewhat derisively) applied to those persons who scampered for the last ferry after whiling away a sociable evening in Greenport. Other, more esoteric interpretations lean toward teutonic origin—an employer named Herr Lacher, for instance, or the word *herrlich*, meaning "splendid", referring somehow to a preponderance of clergymen on Divinity Hill. Be that as it may, the term is jealously perpetuated not only by those who can claim it but often by those who cannot.

Of course the aboriginal natives no longer live here—namely, those Manhanset Indians whose chief, Pogatticut, said his evening prayers on Sunset Rock along the harbor shore near the entrance to the Village. Only a few arrowheads and legends bear meager witness to that era; but they are far more genuine than the bronze plaque erected between the North Ferry parking lot and the Beach Club:

On this spot July 11, 1508
Fell Putikaos
Last of the Sihaqua Indians
Slain by the Norse Viking
Retawerif.

The best way to unravel the mystery of "Putikaos" and "Retawerif" is to read them backward.

The first Europeans to establish firm foothold on the coast of present-day Maine in 1607, and Massachusetts in 1620, ignored New York completely. But in 1637 the Plymouth Colony, at royal behest, ceded what is now Long Island to William Alexander, Earl of Stirling, whose agent, James Farrett, had permission to select 10,000 acres for himself. Wisely he chose Shelter Island; unwisely, he never settled there.

The colonial era actually opened fifteen years later with the arrival of Nathaniel Sylvester, one of a consortium of four sugar merchants of Barbados who bought the island for its fine stands of white oak, suitable for making barrels. Rum business! The agreed price was 1,600 pounds of their principal commodity—sugar—worth about $80. In passing let be noted that in today's real estate market, their investment of one cent per acre would bring a price per acre ranging from $10,000 to $40,000 along the shore.

The new owners were given to understand that the Indians had already been adequately reimbursed for their tribal home, but they found them still in full possession and understandably reluctant to move away. A second purchase was amicably arranged and clear title obtained.

Young Nathaniel Sylvester lost no time in bringing his sixteen-year-old bride from England, or in building a large home for her near the creek that empties into Dering Harbor. It stood next to the present Sylvester Manor, which dates from 1773. Theirs had been an adventurous honeymoon, culminating with a shipwreck in Long Island Sound on the final leg of the voyage. All their household goods, presumably including dowry and wedding gifts, were lost. Soon afterward this compassionate pair—themselves royalist refugees from Cromwellian England—opened their home to some elderly Quakers who had been banished from Boston. In the moving words of John Greenleaf Whittier, they

> ... found
> A peaceful deathbed and a quiet grave
> Where ocean walled, and wiser than his age,
> The Lord of Shelter scorned the bigot's rage.

Later the courageous young couple twice had the honor of entertaining the noted Quaker leader, George Fox, on his visits to America.

Not many years later, the monarchy having been restored, the estate became a manor by an act of the British governor with approval from the crown. By 1673 Nathaniel owned the entire island, thanks to some astute footwork on his part during a Dutch attempt to dislodge the British.

At his death in 1680 Nathaniel's holdings were divided among five sons. The two who eventually gained full control gradually sold off hundreds of acres. From then on, as the land was further divided, the population multiplied—until by 1730 there were twenty families in residence. That was the year in which the handful of widely scattered homesteads became a self-governing town.

Its subsequent growth for well over a century was gradual and unremarkable, except for an interlude during the American Revolution when a British squadron wintered off Hay Beach Point, replenishing their supplies of fuel, food and forage at the expense of angry islanders. After that the inhabitants remained undisturbed until well into the 1800s. Traffic from New York City to Boston via Orient Point ferry bypassed the little island, whose self-sufficient farmers generally used their own boats to get to Southold or Sag Harbor. Only as the Long Island Railroad came to the growing Village of Greenport did attempts to inaugurate a public ferry service succeed.

A really revolutionary change occurred in the 1870s when the island was invaded by two great resort hotels—which is where our story begins. Prospect House and Manhanset House have both long since disappeared but their memory lingers on. Several small and less grandiose establishments continue this strand of "watering place" tradition, but the accent has shifted from summer hotels to summer cottages, which are loosely grouped in unincorporated neighborhoods with names like The Heights, West Neck, Montclair Colony, Westmoreland Farm, Silver Beach, South Ferry Hills, Ram Island, Hay Beach and, of course, the incorporated Village of Dering Harbor.

As is usual in any process of change, there were both gains and losses. This book might be described as an effort to balance the accounts so far as Dering Harbor is concerned. Perhaps the biggest loss has been knowledge of the past. For instance, all records and documents pertaining to the majestic Manhanset House vanished with the hotel itself. A time-consuming search both *for* and *in* surviving brochures and yellowed newspapers, plus considerable research in Town and County records, gradually produced a thin tissue of names, dates and circumstances relating to the spa's more glamorous years. Footnotes have been provided to mark trails already trodden and to invite further exploration. Persistent digging may ultimately reveal the location of Isaac's Grotto or Manhanset Mound!

Only a month before Locust Point—the site of the future Village—was sold to the developers, Henry Wadsworth Longfellow was an honored guest of his Harvard colleague and Cambridge neighbor, Professor Eben Norton Horsford, at Sylvester Manor. To celebrate the nineteenth birthday of Cornelia Horsford, the New England poet planted a shoot of ivy by an old cedar tree, but it was Cornelia's father—though his field was chemistry, not literature—who wrote the verses in honor of the occasion, a "Song of Shelter Island":

On Shelter Island Shore
Is rest forever more.

Chorus: The winds are dead,
      The waves have fled,
       The storm is far away.

The winds have had their day
The waves have ceased to play.

From shingled Hay Beach strand
Behold enchanted land.

In depths of Locust Grove
Fond maidens love to rove.

In Picnic's sheltered dell
The song birds love to dwell.

In Julia's silver mead
The tiny turtles feed.

On Sunset Rock the light
Of maiden's ghost gleams bright

In Hawk's nest perched on high
The young one's merry cry.

Where winds and waters lull
Ward keeps the lone sea gull.

From out his rocky keep
He plunges through the deep.

On old Manhanset mound
Gate of the Hunting Ground

Warriors and chieftains rest
Companions of the blest.

In Isaac's Grotto old
Montauk's sad story told.

So here his resting place
Last of the royal race.

The murmurs of the deep
O'er faithful Afric's sweep.

Can it be that the Isaac mentioned was another poet and a good friend of Longfellow, Isaac McClellan, who spent many seasons in and around Shelter Island, or that the Manhanset Mound of the poem, with its Indian burial ground, is the site of Dering Harbor's water tank?

Chapter II

THE MAGNIFICENT
MANHANSET HOUSE
1870-80

UP UNTIL a century ago, the Village of Dering Harbor was still uninhabited—a tract of two hundred pleasantly wooded acres known as Locust Point. For over two hundred years it had been part of the estate belonging to the Sylvester family and before that it had belonged to the Manhanset Indians.

But in August 1872 a "small group of gentlemen from the East"—that is, Massachusetts rather than New York—formed themselves into the Locust Point Association and bought the tract for $50,000. The legal purchaser and chief member of the group was Erastus P. Carpenter of Foxboro, Massachusetts, a developer who received one-fifth of the purchase price as his fee. A one-page prospectus, issued in the name of the Shelter Island Land Company, offered shares at a par value of $100 and the opportunity to buy two lots on condition that one cottage per year, costing no less than $1,500, be erected.

A few weeks later Mr. Carpenter invited a score of interested investors to view the undeveloped acreage and to discuss the possibilities in a meeting at the Clark Hotel, Greenport's best. Contractors stood ready to cross the channel and start driving piles for a wharf, the indispensable preliminary to any construction on that part of the island. This was delayed by a brief flurry of sentiment in favor of changing the "sight" *(sic)* from Picknic Hollow on the Greenport channel to a location overlooking Dering Harbor.[1] Finally the site on the channel, just above Picknic Hollow, carried the day.

Shortly before Christmas a second meeting of stockholders was convened in New York city at—appropriate touch!—the St. Nicholas Hotel. There a corporation was formed and Locust Point officially became Shelter Island Park. Mr. Erastus Carpenter was elected president. On January 1, 1873 he legally transferred the property to the new company. Little else is known about him except that he was the "originator" of other resort developments, notably the Oak Bluffs Camp Meeting on Martha's Vineyard.[2] His letterhead identifies him as the managing editor of the Kankakee Corporation of Boston, capitalized at $1,000,000. He remained president of the Shelter Island Park Association for about twenty years.

The most important ingredient of the proposed park was to be a large summer hotel whose construction would spawn, so to speak, innumerable "seashore cottages." An over-optimistic timetable called for a July 1 opening; but work on the hotel did not get under way until March, and carpenters were still clambering about the wooden frame in July. Indeed, one man fell from it. Another full year elapsed before the Manhanset House, rising above the trees on the high ground above Greenport channel, was ready to welcome its first guests. For the next forty years it flourished as one of the more renowned watering places along the Atlantic coast.

The time for such vacation resorts had arrived. The 1870s, in the wake of a devastating Civil War, were a strange mixture of affluence and affectation. It was the dawn of the golden age of family hotels, vast wooden chateaux or rambling rustic lodges operated on the so-called American Plan. Full of squeaks and creaks but romantically bordering some secluded mountain lake or the briny deep, they proved to be immensely popular. Scenery was an all-important consideration with, if possible, a slight wigwam flavor. The new deluxe hotel on Shelter Island promptly appropriated the name of the tribe of Indians who two centuries earlier had peacefully relinquished their ancient birthright and retired from the island-surrounded-by-islands.

One of the Manhanset House's very first guests was a special correspondent of the prestigious *Brooklyn Eagle*, writing under the pen name of John Scotus. He marveled at all he saw i "Two and a half years ago Shelter Island was as little known to the people of Brooklyn as some island of minor importance in the Pacific Ocean." Enthusiastically he described the Manhanset House: "opened for the first time this summer... quite late in the season... rapidly filling up with guests... situated among locust trees to the East and a denser grove of oaks and ash to the West." Each bedroom, he reported, had a parlor and the beds were the best he ever slept in—in a hotel. Also, "Three or four cottages are being erected."[3]

It is generally supposed that 1873 was the year when the Manhanset House first opened its doors. Not so. Although the exact date—probably some time in mid-July—is still unknown, the correct year is definitely 1874, confirmed inadvertently by an 1883 news source stating that the hotel opened "nine years ago."[4] By early August the dynamic young manager reportedly had "his share" of guests, about two hundred of them.[5] But in an article datelined July 26, the same *Eagle-eyed* reporter wrote that "the chief attraction here now is the new and elegant hotel which was opened for the first time this summer and which, notwithstanding the severity of the times, is already well filled with a class of guests not surpassed in culture and refinement."[6] The 200-foot frontage, the 200-foot ell, the deep piazzas—verandas, of course—and the asphalt walks, all command his attention.

The reporter's enthusiasm for the superior accommodations can best be grasped by comparing his account with that of a colleague who had traveled as far as Greenport four years earlier.

The Long Island Railroad terminates on a little pier built out into the water, whence you foot it to the Peconic Hotel. I went to bed with a Rush light in a room with no lock on the door and no door to speak of either. The march of modern improvement had placed a bell in the tavern, and it was hung in the main hall where all boarders could get to it. This was not bad, the only consequence being a knock on the door every ten minutes during the night to know if I had rung—my door being next to the aforesaid bell [but] I had one of the best breakfasts I ever swallowed, delicious clams, delicate watercress, with butter sweet as honey and yellow as the sunrise I had seen.[7]

The major coup of the new spa's inaugural weeks was having everyone on the Brooklyn Yacht Club cruise in attendance at the very first Saturday night hop. Let the diarist of the fleet rise to his own inimitable climax:

Immediately after 8 bells the little steam yacht, plying as a ferryboat between the Island and Greenport, was taxed to her utmost to carry the numerous yachtsmen and ladies of the village across the harbor... At 9 o'clock the hop was in full progress, and a jollier crowd I never saw. Yacht clubs have enjoyed similar scenes, but never before had such entire *éclat* attended like hopicular arrangements.[8]

Before the end of that first year the owners were preparing to add a 150-foot extension to the hotel. Why not? When Erastus Carpenter paid his first visit to the finished hotel in September, on his return from a long trip to Europe, he was royally greeted by an illumination of the grounds in his honor and a serenade by the Greenport Cornet Band.[9] The prophecy of one commentator who foresaw that "in five years from now 5,000 summer tourists will camp in hotels, cottages or tents on Shelter Island,"[10] seemed entirely capable of fulfilling itself. Soon the annex overlooking the channel was remodeled into additional guest apartments and its bowling alleys were relegated to a new recreation building behind the hotel.

Manhanset vs. Menhaden

But the budding summer resort business still had to contend with competition of quite another sort. As one observant traveler was quick to note, "The crowning industry of the people here seems to be the 'manufacture of fish,' so called. They certainly succeed in manufacturing a most villainous stench and if smells are good fertilizer, I cannot conceive of a country where broom corn would grow higher, or cereal yield more bushels to the acre, than in the vicinity of Greenport — breathing pestilence and corruption, all over the country."[11]

These comments were also applicable to Shelter Island. The prevailing breezes were neither pine-scented nor salt-laden, as they wafted from "fish factories" that had established beachheads at such widely-scattered locations as the base of White Hill, the foot of Burns Avenue, Ram Head, Coecles Harbor and Hay Beach. So far as the new Shelter Island Park was concerned, the most noisome were those on Chequit Point, site of the present Yacht Club, and at Dinah's Rock. No resort hotel caught in such an aromatic crossfire could long endure.

Such was the bunker industry so-called, that flourished at this time. Indeed, there was a Bunker City growing like a tumor on the shores of Coecles Harbor. The business was based on great schools of menhaden or mossbunker, an inedible kind of herring, valuable only for oil used in paints and the leftover scrap, whose high nitrogen content the Indians had long ago learned to make use of. Following the aboriginal example, white settlers spread the decaying fish on their cropland—using as many as 15,000 fish per acre. Soon the farmers were banding together to catch fish for this purpose, and before long the commercial possibilities of this smelly operation—at from 50 to 75 cents per thousand—was recognized.

By 1881 there would be nearly a hundred factories in Suffolk County, employing 2,800 men and relying on 286 sailing vessels and 73 steamboats to bring in huge quantities of fish. Extracting the oil by cooking was done in large open sheds—whence the odor.

The one person who is given major credit for preventing Shelter Island from becoming a sort of Smelter Island was Eben N. Horsford, the influential lord of Sylvester Manor, who had sold Locust Point to Erastus Carpenter. Control of the estate had come to him through his marriage to Mary L'Hommedieu Gardiner, a lineal descendant of Nathaniel Sylvester, the original settler. Already over sixty years of age at this time, he was president of the Rumford Baking Powder Company as well as professor of chemistry at Harvard, and had thirty remunerative patents to his credit. He had devised marching rations for use by the army; General Grant had placed an order for 500,000. Among other distinctions, Horsford was president of the Wellesley College board of visitors and official U. S. representative to the Vienna Exposition of 1873. In fact, he had consulted with the Manhanset House architect, Clark, shortly before leaving for Austria, where he personally explained some of the American exhibits to Emperor Franz Josef—and suffered the embarrassment of having his hat blow off and fly over His Imperial Majesty's head. But Horsford's special passion was the pursuit of clues authenticating the early visits of Leif Ericson and his Vikings to the New England shores.

Each spring the arrival of the Horsfords in their handsome barouche, drawn by a matched team of horses, to take up seasonal residence at the Manor was a notable event. Virtually the only other summer visitors during the 1860s were the descendants of another old Island family, the Havens, who had kept their old homestead too.[12] The ferry trip itself was quite enough to daunt the average traveler, not to mention the primitive state of the highways both on and off the Island. However, public transportation was improving, holidaying was becoming popular and Professor Horsford possessed the twin attributes of vision and energy. He not only embellished his own estate with better roads and invited the Islanders to enjoy them, but was said to have been responsible for building a lookout tower on White Hill, the highest part of the Island—as though to lift the sights of his contemporaries to the level of an enraptured metropolitan reporter who reporter who saw "Great Peconic Bay stretched out to the left and Gardiner's Bay to the right; the Sound glittering in the morning sun on the one side and the broad Atlantic on the other; the picturesque village of Greenport in front and the whole of Shelter Island at our feet."[13]

The truth is that the tower had been built by the owner of the land, one Captain Osborn. A visitor from Massachusetts who huffed and puffed up the "gravelly ascent" and mounted the "wretched framework"— apparently in a stiff breeze—pronounced the tower "unsafe for even one person to climb." He conceded, however, that "even the Bay of Naples could not exceed in loveliness" the view from the top.[14] It should be added that by the following summer a "strong and substantial tower" had replaced the "wretched" one.[15] Perhaps Professor Horsford instigated that.

In any event, the professor and the view from the tower both had a part in persuading some Brooklyn Methodists to buy three hundred acres from the Squire Chase estate for a summer resort and camp-meeting ground. Besides White Hill itself, this tract included the rugged peninsula known as Prospect, which today is called Shelter Island Heights. Indeed, the Brooklyn group had already opened their big Prospect Hotel when Squire Horsford agreed to sell Locust Point to the Massachusetts gentlemen. A year later Horsford bought out the fertilizer plant at Dinah's Rock in order to transform that beach and some of its buildings into a picnic grove which for many years was to be a powerful magnet for excursion steamers up and down the coast. Especially the carousel!

In many respects this was the closing phase of a war already won. Mounting sentiment against the odorous industry had culminated in an order from the Board of Health to the Island's factories "to discontinue all manufacturing of fish oil, fish scrap and fish guano" by November 10, 1871. The plant on Hay Beach obligingly burned down at about this time. Those remaining were obliged to remove all "badsmelling & noisome compounds" from the Island by April 1872.

To issue this order took courage, since Long Island had been gripped by the "oil fever"; 75 million fish had been seined in the previous year, enticing greedy imaginations with visions of wealth. In 1871 alone a catch of 124 million mossbunker yielded 600,000 gallons of oil and 12,603 tons of guano, bringing $616,000 to Suffolk County.

On the other hand, the agreement with the Brooklyn Methodists had clearly called for discontinuing the nearby plants, two of which bracketed the Prospect peninsula. It was either—or! The issue was hotly debated, and some of the factories were understandably recalcitrant; but Professor Horsford and the Camp Meeting Association "did not abate any of their hostility." By June 1872 the president of the Association was able to announce that the nearby factories had been removed and the new resort grounds would open July 4 as scheduled. As luck would have it, Gardiner's Bay that same year was "alive" with menhaden, a "solid mass of fish." "Never were more seen within its shores."[16] Shortly thereafter several vessels including an old quarantine ship from New York harbor were enterprisingly outfitted as floating fish factories in Gardiner's Bay. But so far as the Island's shores were concerned, the die had been cast and negotiations for the second large resort hotel could begin.

Boston's Culture? Brooklyn's Religion?

Plans for the two undertakings were virtually identical. Each envisaged a big hotel surrounded by a close-packed cottage colony in a leafy grove. Both were designed as family resorts, not simply including children but envisaging the whole community as one big family. As the dewy-eyed promotional flyer put it, "It is obvious that this cottage system of living in communities will enable families to secure, at moderate cost, the health and exemption from care of camp life; and unite with them the neatness and comfort of a furnished house, the refinement of carpets, pictures and flowers, and the independence and safety of home."

The earliest private cottages were actually kitchenless in the expectation that everybody would eat in a common dining room. And, of course, the hotel would provide all the entertainment, from costume parties to church services. This, the prevalent summer-resort pattern, was followed by both the Prospect House and the Manhanset House, whose respective peninsulas shared, and were separated by, one of the finest natural harbors on the North Atlantic coast.

From the very beginning, the two parallel ventures each had a distinctive character and a natural rivalry toward the other. How could it have been otherwise? Squire Chase had dreamed of an idyllic city of sobriety—to be called Sobrie—rising from his woodland acres; but he never lived to see it. The development of Prospect when it finally came would no doubt have pleased him. Apparently it was inspired by the example of Oak Bluffs, a cottage city on Martha's Vineyard in which Erastus Carpenter had been involved. Enterprises of this kind were an authentic part of America's romantic and religious revival in the closing decades of the nineteenth century. Their most popular form, the camp meeting, rapidly became institutionalized in summer resorts, of which Asbury Park and Ocean Grove on the Jersey coast were outstanding examples.

It was the heyday of Dwight L. Moody and Ira Sankey. The Shelter Island Grove and Camp Meeting Association—to give Prospect its official name—must be seen as an integral part of a national movement, which culminated at Chautauqua. Sankey himself visited the Island, as George Whitefield had over a century earlier, and several of Brooklyn's most eloquent preachers—Storrs, Behrends, Coe—now built fine cottages on White Hill, which thereupon became known as Divinity Hill. Revival services in a grove south of the hotel were enlivened, we are told, by a Scot named John Parker, "a shouting Methodist of the old-fashioned type... especially when soliciting for good causes."[17]

Lest this aura of sanctity—replacing the odor of fish—become so overwhelming as to repel prospective vacationers, a counterattack was mounted:

> I should like to try and correct an impression prevalent in Brooklyn, which I am sure is an erroneous one, relative to the habits and customs of those living in and visiting this part of Shelter Island. The very name of Shelter Island has become almost synonymous for Puritanical restraint. This is a great mistake... Those who landed at the Prospect Hotel pier suddenly found themselves in as gay a place as could have been found. The ladies had laid aside their croquet implements, sent their rosy-cheeked children away for the night, and were seated about the grounds and on the piazzas enjoying the cool evening air. Within a hundred feet of the pier was a well-patronized bowling alley and close by it Major Schroeder stood playing at billiards (and losing), and Mr. President French at bagatelle... It was up at the hotel, however, that gaiety had reached its height. The parlors were resonant with music and giddy with waltzing couples. I never saw more unalloyed enjoyment in my life at a seaside watering place. What the secret is I don't know, but the 500 or 600 people now here are more like one family than 150 families.[18]

The same writer went on to say that the gaiety may have been the reaction to the camp meeting which had just closed. It had lasted two weeks, with preaching sessions morning, afternoon and evening. Special trains brought in additional crowds and preachers. Steamers from New Haven off-loaded a thousand people one August weekend in 1874 and 1,700 the next. The revival leaders—or some of them, whom the reporter derided as "unmuscular Christians"—caused the temporary closing of the bowling alleys, "which bring fresh blood and life to the brain, and strength and substance to the muscles." At the same time he noted with approval that "no amount of money will buy any sort of strong drink in this settlement. Its members get along very well without. They have had no serious sickness among them, no drowning, or other casualties or accidents. In fact, after a day or two's discipline, the moderate drinker will find absolute enjoyment under this regulation. Some find it a little hard at first. I have seen Brooklynites go 6 or 7 miles by the Greenport ferry-boat, as they said, to get the fresh air. Now just think of that as an excuse made at a place like this."[19] Such was the nature of the "great moral watering place" which was "fast becoming fashionable."[20]

Fewer eyewitnesses have left reports of the Manhanset House but it may be assumed that both piety and temperance lodged there too, albeit not quite so ostentatiously. Its rates were slightly higher and its tone somewhat more secular. Whereas one particular week's reporting from Prospect either reviewed or announced the sermons of six different ministers, the main item from the rival establishment ran as follows: "On Thursday last week the guests of Manhanset went on the steam yacht Mystic to Purple Jenning's grove and had a clam bake. Judging from the 'straw' left on the grounds, they had a good time."[21]

The difference between Manhanset and Prospect comes to vivid life in a long article in the *New York Tribune* on May 15, 1883, reprinted later that month in the *Suffolk Weekly Times*. Here are some excerpts:

> The long and silent winter has been succeeded by the bustle of busy excitement that presages the "season*"... Everybody is pleased... "Everybody" on Shelter Island in winter is a somewhat comprehensive term; but in summer it is stretched with a vengeance. Everybody then exists here in two editions, to use a technical expression—in two bound volumes as it were, the one of Boston, the other of Brooklyn make. That of the City of Churches is the more varied and interesting; that of the Hub the more exclusive and quite the more aristocratic Perhaps it is the difference between religion, perhaps the style of the two towns.

> The men from Brooklyn were Methodists and bent on camp-meetings. Honest John French was at their head; they settled on the old Chase homestead... Their purchase embraced the highest hills on the island and the finest views... The Association put up a hotel... a chapel, a caserne for summer boarders and five cottages. Not to be outdone, the Boston folk did likewise. They spent $85,000* in building the Manhanset House and put up five cottages, but left out the chapel. The hotel was an ambitious affair and is to this day the finest in all Eastern Long Island. Then both concerns cut up their acres into building lots, 2,000 each, and offered them to the world. Methodism and the clergy stood by

---

*Other reports give the figure as $150,000.

Brooklyn nobly, even when camp-meetings were abandoned after a few years, and in the race between religion and culture, religion came out a long way ahead...

... the Boston establishment over the way has flourished but not increased. To the original five cottages that cluster behind the Manhanset House none have been added until this Spring when New York has come to the rescue in the person of one of its citizens who is now building a summer house there. Of the two hotels that formed the kernels of settlements the Manhanset was always the more "high-toned" and expensive, as it is the handsomer; but the preponderance of popular favor has been with the democratic side of the inlet, where blue shirts are allowable and fun is at a premium over dignity... Both hotels are always crowded in the season.**

The tide had unmistakably turned. Shelter Island's fertilizer factories were on their way out, beginning with the one at the foot of White Hill, in what became Scudder Cove, and ending with Bunker City, whose immigrant laborers occasionally imbibed the "poison" in Greenport's waterfront bars and came home on the last ferry to the Manhanset wharf, where their raucous singing of Democratic songs annoyed the hotel's Republican guests. The resort industry was thriving. Various other development plans—at West Neck, for example—were announced and boarding houses were burgeoning to accommodate visitors of more modest needs. By 1883 even the Island's farmers were busily reaping their own harvest of summer guests at a sensible $8 per week.

Opening Up The Island

These changes inevitably brought still other changes to an insular community that had expanded very gradually over the last three hundred years, from one small family to about eight hundred permanent residents, all of whom lived frugally from the soil and the sea. Ferry service, for instance, took on a new significance. Less than thirty years before the building of the hotels, a young man named Jonathan Preston had made several efforts, none of them successful, to inaugurate a regular Green-port-Shelter Island-Sag Harbor service with sailing boats—the first six feet, the next eighteen feet, and the last twenty-three feet long. Those were the days when carriages went by raft and horses swam, tethered astern. A decade later, Captain Preston obtained a state ferry charter and built the first dock in Dering Harbor.[22]

In the 1870s, thanks to the steam engine, more dependable ways of reaching Shelter Island, and filling its hotels, became possible. Train service from New York to Greenport was already excellent—two hours flat from Flatbush Station in Brooklyn. With the advent of the hotels, a triangular ferry service from Greenport to Prospect to Manhanset was instituted. The first vessel to provide

---

**Board and room at the Prospect was $15 per person per week; at the Manhanset it was $18.

this vastly improved service was the *Cambria*, a fishing boat converted to steam only a couple years before; it was destined to ply the route for twenty years. It was owned and operated by Frederick Chase Beebe, an Islander, who after selling out in 1876 went into boat-building in Greenport.* To supplement the train and ferry, the overnight steamers *Escort* and *W. W. Coit* brought whole households-families with servants—direct from New York City to Shelter Island with bag and baggage, horse and carriage, to spend the summer.

The next change, logically, affected Shelter Island's roads. Hotel guests could not be expected to spend all their leisure time in rocking chairs on the broad piazzas. The owners of large yachts, whose handsome craft filled the harbor, were in a class by themselves; but even they enjoyed a change of pace, especially when becalmed. The Prospect House opened an Entertainment Hall near its beach with indoor games, a restaurant and an ice cream saloon. Manhanset had its Amusement Hall—billiards, bowling, etc.—next to the hotel. But all this was still not enough.

There were other things to be done and sights to be seen: for example, a "plague" of tramps which overran the Island in 1877, or the annual gypsy caravan which arrived via the South Ferry and was quickly escorted to the North Ferry— not to mention the team of horses that met with a grisly accident in 1879, when they were caught in the turning blades of the old grist mill and ended, it was said, with their hooves in the air; or what was left of the Lookout Tower on White Hill after a bad storm demolished it that same year. Such things had to be witnessed at first hand as part of the summer's souvenirs. Before the end of the first decade, a livery franchise was granted to a local entrepreneur, who supplied horses, both fast and slow, as well as "smart turnouts." Then a branch livery was set up near Prospect ferry slip—a regular rent-a-carriage, drive-it-yourself operation. Hence the need for more and better roads for enjoying scenic views "not exceeded by any watering place south of Mt. Desert."[23]

Those were the days before Shelter Island had highways. The approach to Manhanset on the landward-side, for example, was over a rough wagon road through fields and meadows which were well fenced in. Such barriers were annoying to sightseers, even after young volunteers had seized the opportunity of riding along to remove the bars—for a small tip of course. The first and almost the only public highway on the Island seems to have been the link between the South Ferry and Boisseau's, which ran from Crescent Beach to Southold before the service to Greenport was inaugurated.

After Captain Preston had installed docking facilities in Dering Harbor, resident Islanders soon pressed for public access roads to shorten the route for shipping farm produce direct to the railhead in the increasingly important Village of Greenport. When the Camp Meeting Association bought the ferry company for $4,250 in 1873, the Town sought an agreement on the year-round use of the

---

*With Capt. C. H. McClellan, head of the U. S. Life-Saving Service, he developed the famous Beebe-McClellan self-bailing, self-righting boat for rescue work from open beaches.

Prospect wharf but was for some reason rebuffed. The ire of the natives was further aroused by the doubling of the 12-cent passenger fare during the four winter months. The Manhanset House, on the other hand, offered use of its dock in the off season, from September 15 to June 15, provided the Town would share maintenance costs and not use the terminal building for storage. The townspeople declared themselves "much pleased with the liberal and friendly spirit of the Shelter Island Park Association" in contrast to that of the Brooklyn company,[24] and were "almost unanimously" in favor of building a road "from the center of the Island" to the Manhanset dock. This road, which no doubt followed an old lane across the fields, is known today as Manhanset Road.[25]

At about the same time, Professor Horsford had "a very fine avenue laid out through his place to connect with the Manhanset House by a bridge, which will shorten the distance between that place and Prospect about 2 miles; adding much to the convenience of procuring teams from the livery stables."[26] That avenue probably followed the east side of Gardiner's Creek and crossed a bridge at Julia Havens' Creek (see chart). Winthrop Road was not opened up until 1881; whereupon at a cost of $350, a bridge was thrown across Gardiner's Creek, further reducing the distance between the two hotels. Still later—about 1884—Professor Horsford laid a new road from Gardiner's Creek to Coecles Harbor; presumably it is the Cobbetts Lane of today.

Rowing—Not Rocking—the Boat

Regardless of greater freedom of movement provided by improved roads, the social life of summer visitors still centered in and around the two big hotels. By day one could saunter in the groves or go for a swim—which, for the ladies at least, amounted to little more than getting wet while standing in the water decorously clad from head to toe. Manhanset House maintained a long string of bath houses—not in front of the hotel where the vessels came and went, but on the Dering Harbor side away from the strong tidal current.[27] Prospect House maintained its bathing facilities where the peppermint-striped beach club still stands.

According to contemporary newspaper accounts the most popular pastime for young people on warm summer evenings was to congregate in rowboats out on the water. Large fleets of them known "sharpies," were available for hire. A reporter saw as many as fifty such boats being rowed around, heartily endorsed the custom as being "the best exercise" for the chest muscles, thus warding off the danger of consumption.[28] The scene is evoked in the following paragraph:

> Boats decorated with ñags, with parties of singers, who make "music upon the waters"; boats filled with quiet couples, who row and woo; boats

filled with children who make the "welkin ring" with their gleeful laughter; boats with rollicking and boisterous boys, whose vociferous shouts echo from hill to hill; the boat with the patent screw propeller, owned by a gentleman from Elizabeth, who quietly sits and plays his flute, while he easily turns the crank that propels him, these are scenes and sounds upon Deerings* Harbor every pleasant evening, and now when the moon adds her lustre to the scene, the sport continues late into the night.[29]

Were there no complaints?

To enliven things still more, Friday nights at Manhanset were usually given over to performances, largely by amateurs. Fulsome reports of these events appeared in the ensuing edition of the local news. The Prospect Chapel, incidentally, had a somewhat different idea for Friday evenings. A "series of select entertainments"—including organ, male glee club and readings—"will be chaste and thoroughly enjoyable." On August 3, 1878, for instance, the program featured Miss Abrota S. North of Brooklyn with the assistance of Miss Zilpa I. Hazlet and Miss Lizzie M. Figgis. The names alone are chaste and enjoyable.

Both hotels had their orchestras for dinner music every evening and for the Saturday night hop. It is said that the Manhanset House ensemble also played at teatime in the pavilion overlooking the bathing beach.

Sundays were quite another matter. A decorous quiet prevailed. Services of worship "for those who wish to attend" were frequently held in the Manhanset grove, weather permitting. If not, they were conducted in the parlor. When there was no "Reverend Gentleman" among the guests—which happened rarely—a layman would conduct the service. In the evening the orchestra turned its talents to sacred music. Prospect soon had its attractive frame chapel built about 1875, which is still in use each summer. Back in 1879, three services were scheduled each Sunday: Sabbath School at 11 A.M., Preaching at 3:30 and Praise Service at 8 P.M. There was never any lack of vacationing ministers to man the Prospect pulpit; usually they were sufficiently numerous to supply the old Presbyterian and new Episcopal pulpits as well, and the Manhanset parlor too.

Of much greater concern to some people were the changes in standards and values which Shelter Island's new career as a vacation resort tended to introduce. A local reporter summed up the situation in an end-of-the-season dispatch: "Our summer visitors have nearly all left and our Island people are now busily engaged in ridding themselves of the demoralizing influences which have been so sure to follow in the footsteps of those who make their home in the country during the warm weather. We sincerely hope it will not require a work of nine months this time before our people become church-going and law-abiding citizens."[30]

By the end of the 1870s Shelter Island, whether it liked it or not, was well on its way to becoming an established summer resort to which thousands of vacationers were flocking. After all, it possessed "every attraction that distinguishes Newport or Long Branch."[31] Even the menhaden cooperated by moving farther south along the Jersey coast, taking the fishing fleet and factories with them. Indeed, within twenty years the arrival of boatloads of manure from the streets of New York City at Mr. Artemas Ward's dock near the South Ferry would be a newsworthy item! He and certain other gentlemen farmers joined the Islanders in promoting agriculture with emphasis on potatoes, tomatoes, cauliflower, turnips and lima beans—not just for local consumption but for export. Eventually farming went the way of fishing as a dominant occupation, but its decline was gradual.

All in all, Shelter Island did well in the 1870s when it began turning into a summer resort. Despite subsequent changes, much of its idyllic quality has been preserved by succeeding generations of sentimentally shrewd summer and winter inhabitants. It might even be argued that the loss of the big hotels, after they had fulfilled that purpose, was a blessing in disguise. This, at any rate, is how the cottage colony that is now the Village of Dering Harbor came into being.

Chapter III

GINGERBREAD GALORE 1880-90

WHEN SHELTER ISLAND'S most elegant resort hotel went up in flames, first in 1896 and again in 1910, its records were apparently incinerated too. Nevertheless, by sifting the ashes—that is, all the fragments of data from available contemporary newspapers, brochures, etc.—a good deal of the hotel's history and that of its early cottage community can be recaptured. The resultant mosaic of information, although incomplete, offers tantalizing glimpses into the earliest days of the future Village.

It will be recalled that a reporter's firsthand account of the newly opened Manhanset House in the summer of 1874 mentioned "three or four cottages" being built in conjunction with the hotel. Here is the first clue to the beginnings of the subsequent Village. A very early pictorial advertisement of the hotel, now mounted and hanging in the Village board room, shows four cottages, only one of which is still in existence. What became of the other three, assuming that they were indeed built? Every vestige of them has long since disappeared.

Among the dry-plate photographs left by Dr. Fowler, the hotel's first resident physician, is one of an unfinished building, identified as a "haunted house" that stood "near the hotel". Even earlier is a pen-and-ink drawing of the first Manhanset House by J. Bonney, which shows a small house to the west of the new hotel. There is no other evidence, pictorial or otherwise, that a building stood so close to the tip of Locust Point.

Writing sixty years later, the mayor of the Village states that "three small, unplastered cottages" were erected at the same time as the hotel for three of the major stockholders of the Shelter Island Park Company— namely, Thomas H. Wood, Virgil C. Pond and Henry K. Motley. Unfortunately, the mayor did not indicate the source of his information. The name of the third owner is, as we shall see, almost certainly incorrect; possibly that owner was in fact Erastus Carpenter.*

It is evident that cottages formed an integral part of the original Manhanset plan. Hundreds of them were envisioned; but only about a dozen had been built before 1890. Although most of these survive, it is not easy to determine accurately when and in what sequence they were built or by whom. Some were clearly intended for personal use by individuals connected with the hotel

*The only previous historical account of the Village consists of an unpublished, 25-page essay by the second mayor, Charles Lane Poor. A yellowed typescript, dated

(officers of the corporation, for example), others as income-producing investments. Normally such questions can be answered by recourse to public tax records; but unfortunately the Town of Shelter Island during those early years carried the whole Park as one taxable unit, taking no notice of the individual cottages as they were built.

From circumstantial evidence, including size and structural design, it is a safe assumption that the three "unplastered" cottages to which Mayor Poor later referred are the two-story "gingerbread" houses still standing near the foot of Gardiner Way.[1] They were once identical. None of the three was built later than 1874, making them the oldest cottages extant in Dering Harbor. One of them— but which one?—appears in the upper lefthand corner of the early advertisement hanging in the Village board room. And in one of them, a crude inscription was scratched on the back of a stair riser in the hall closet by a William Morgan of London, England stating that he had labored for Queen Victoria!

Despite considerable modernization, all three structures remain authentically Victorian. A major and very early improvement seems to have been the addition of a full-fledged kitchen with back stairs leading to a servant's room and toilet, lending further weight to the conclusion that these were the cottages mentioned by the reporter in 1874. Apparently the original expectation that all meals would either be eaten in or served from a single dining room proved impractical or unenforceable, and after a few years was quietly abandoned by both hotels. None of the later cottages, whether at Manhanset or Prospect, appears ever to have been without a kitchen.[2] Incidentally, the very first cottages connected with the Prospect Hotel seem to have been the three cedar-shingled cottages along the shore near the North Ferry, easily identified by the their hexagonal kitchen annexes.

As for the individuals for whom the small, unplastered cottages were first constructed, independent evidence supports Mayor Poor's contention that at least two of them were indeed privately built, for Thomas Wood and Virgil Pond. As already indicated, all shareholders of the Park Association were entitled to select two lots for every ten shares of stock and were expected to erect cottages, a stipulation that was later contained in some of the deeds.[3] Perhaps three of the major officers and shareholders, hoping to set a good example for investors, simply ordered three identical cottages to be built at their expense. Whether they actually inhabited them for any length of time poses another question.

The first known occupant of any of the three houses is Arthur O. Headley of Newark, New Jersey, who rented the Pond cottage at the foot of Setauket Avenue for "several seasons" before buying it in 1883.[4] Headley brought it from Virgil S. Pond, who had acquired the lot from the association for $125 and whose name stands second on the lengthy list of persons to whom the very first deeds

---

August 1933, was found in New York City among the papers of the third mayor, William O'Conor, whose son kindly returned it to the Village archives in 1974. The document, despite a few errors, is very valuable both for factual data and personal recollections.

were conveyed in January 1875. This information suggests that Pond probably built his cottage in 1873 or 1874 but that there was considerable delay in recording the first batch of deeds. Headley enlarged his holding two years later by buying the adjacent lot from Thomas Wood for $400,[5] and the property remained in the possession of the Headley family thereafter for a total of forty years.

The first known resident of the adjoining cottage on Setauket Avenue—now Gardiner Way—was Manhanset's summer physician, Dr. George B. Fowler of New York City, who undoubtedly occupied it in 1884, if not even earlier, and returned to it for many subsequent seasons. The Fowlers and the Headleys played leading roles in the social life and amateur entertainment at the hotel. The actual owner of the Fowler cottage, however, was Thomas Wood, who in 1884 bought the vacant lot from his fellow shareholders, Motley and Pond, for $500.[6] To this lot he moved the present cottage from its original site, only 60 feet distant—that is, the width of a standard lot. Like his fellow stockholder, Virgil Pond, he does not seem to have lived in it himself, at least after it was moved. Nevertheless, he or his widow remained in control of the house for a total of forty-five years. Meanwhile, in 1890, he built a larger cottage "for his own use"[7] in the place of still another one which he had been occupying. The latter stood closer to the hotel, and Wood converted it into a drugstore for the community. Soon, as we shall see, Thomas Wood was to succeed Erastus Carpenter as president of the corporation.

The history of the third "gingerbread" cottage[8] is even more complex. It was neither built nor owned by Henry Motley, as Mayor Poor suggests; possibly the builder was Erastus Carpenter, the initial developer, but he appears not to have been the original owner of the two lots on which it stands. Incidentally, Mayor Poor also gives 1873 as the year when they were constructed. This would be correct only if the cottages preceded the completion of the hotel by a full year—as is by no means inconceivable, since their construction was simpler and would have proceeded more rapidly, permitting the officers of the association to supervise progress of the larger work.

A Yacht Is not a Cottage

By closing one's eyes, it is possible to form a clear mental picture of the first Manhanset colony. A wide path climbs sharply away from the ferry wharf on Greenport channel toward the broad piazzas of the hotel. Another path—a boardwalk—winds gently downward, from the hotel through the tall trees, to the three Victorian cottages near the bathing beach on the Dering Harbor side. A few utility buildings huddle unobtrusively along the wagon road behind the hotel, or out of sight in the woods. That is all there was. And so it remained for

Stuart W. Herman

Main Building of First Manhanset House, 1874-1896

Hotel's Bathing Beach on Dering Harbor with pavilion for tea and music

Looking over Dering Harbor toward Prospect Point

the first nine years, except that on the bluff to the east of the hotel a longish, turreted structure, containing bowling alleys, was added. The Manhanset House itself was flourishing but the proposed cottage colony merely marked time. A lot of lots were sold, but no houses built.

One compensation was the large number of yachts in the water, far exceeding the number of cottages on the shore. The New York Yacht Club fleet regularly dropped anchor in the harbor during its summer cruise. Whenever an impressive flotilla arrived, "people turned out by the hundreds and remained for hours, looking at the handsome specimens of naval architecture. At night lanterns, then fireworks, blazed from every boat... and the hotel replied in kind."[9] In midsummer 1886 the steamer *Cygnus* arrived, with 150 members and guests of the New York Yacht Club, followed by thirteen "costly and handsome yachts," which of course evoked a cannon salute, more fireworks and a festive ball. Next day a brass band headed a parade to the dock to bid the fleet farewell.[10] ° These visits soon led, as we shall see, to the establishment of a yacht club "station" next to the hotel's bathing beach.

But a transient yacht in the harbor is not quite the same as a permanent cottage on land. Why should the number of summer homes be multiplying around Prospect House but remain static in the shadow of Manhanset? What had happened to the surveyor's projected vision of hundreds of "seashore cottages," each costing no less than $1,500, on those 60-by-100-foot lots along dozens of winding streets with colorful Indian names?[11] Many lots had indeed been sold during those first few years to people who hesitated or, as speculators, never intended to build. Their names do not reappear in subsequent records, except for the resale of their unimproved property to one or more of the principal stockholders, usually Motley and Pond. Many of the absentee landlords passively held on to one or a dozen lots deep in the woods, where prices stood well below $100 each and where to this day no roads or cottages have been built.

By 1879 a more aggressive and imaginative corporate leadership had asserted itself. Thomas Wood replaced Erastus Carpenter as president of the company and swept in like a new broom. An article in the *Suffolk Weekly Times*, dated May 24, states that the "new owners" of the Manhanset House had arrived and "will proceed at once to have several cottages built" by Boston contractors, "also a large Amusement Hall, ice house and stables." In June these cottages were reported to be under construction, but the report seems to have been premature. However, some "large and commodious" stables were near completion and a livery franchiser, Seth Raynor, was promising "smart turnouts" to his discriminating clients. Also, a new ice house guaranteed the safe storage of hundreds of tons of ice, brought down from Maine aboard three-masted schooners. The formal announcement of the early arrival of Admiral Porter,

USN, and his family was designed to serve notice to the world at large that the hotel could assure its guests of a distinguished clientele. By mid-July Postmaster James of New York City had arrived, followed by Postmaster General Key, who came to the inauguration of Manhanset's own post office, to be staffed by a postmaster, an assistant postmaster and two clerks.

Whether all these improvements warrant the journalistic conclusion that new owners had taken charge is subject to interpretation. What happened was that Virgil S. Pond, who held a mortgage of $60,000 on the hotel, obtained a foreclosure order in 1879 and waived judgment for one dollar, provided that control of the hotel and its five acres, with wharf, be turned over to Henry Motley and Virgil C. Pond.* At the same time the two partners, Motley and Pond, had been buying up lots from disappointed investors, and they now proceeded to buy eighty-six more lots from the corporation for a lump sum of $10,000.

Effective control of the whole Shelter Island Park corporation having thus changed hands, some new policies were introduced. The actual management of the hotel itself was entrusted as before to professionals, usually men who operated first-class hotels in New York or Florida during the winter. The most significant change was the separation of the hotel's fifteen acres from the remaining one hundred eighty-five acres of unimproved land, thus dividing the ongoing operation of the hotel from the further development of real estate.

At this point the name of Henry K. Motley crops up again in the local news:

> Mr. Henry K. Motley, Treasurer of the Shelter Island Park Association, has contracted with C. Jetter of Riverhead to build for him a handsome cottage on his lot near Manhanset House for his own occupancy. This is a step in the right direction and we hope that the time is not far distant when others who own lots adjoining this fine hotel will show the same spirit of enterprise by building many more. Although this magnificent House has always since its erection in 1873 enjoyed the reputation of being located on one of the finest spots along our Eastern Long Island coast, there has long been an indifferent feeling among those holding its stock about the necessity of enlarging the place by building more cottages in order that a greater number of people may be brought together.[12]

Apparently Henry Motley had never before owned a cottage here. Now he received full credit for setting an overdue example. The *Suffolk Weekly Times* pointed out a few weeks later that "to the five original cottages that cluster behind the Manhanset House none have been added until this spring."[13] The mention of the "five cottages," incidentally, seems to indicate the existence not only of the three "gingerbread" houses but of two others which must have stood

---

*Both a Virgil S. and a Virgil C. Pond are involved in the early real estate records. Virgil S. Pond seems to have been the principal stockholder; Virgil C.

closer to the hotel, perhaps on the lawn now graced by the Village flagpole. Two such buildings are known to have occupied that space, one of which served variously as staff residence, auxiliary hotel office, and post office, eventually becoming the first Village hall. The other served *inter alia* as a drug store.

Be that as it may, the first cottage to have been built after an interval of nine years is now clearly identified as the one that stands by the bend of Shore Road just above the old bathing beach.[14] For its first half century this house was owned by men who were intimately connected with the hotel corporation or the Dering Harbor golf club and was sometimes mistakenly regarded as one of the Manhanset guest cottages.

A Building Boomlet, but No Stables

Motley's action triggered a small construction boom. Two more houses quickly followed his, both erected by islanders along the Dering Harbor shore built at intervals of few hundred feet. These were the Bateman and Cartwright cottages and both were obviously rental properties. The former was put up just one year after Motley's by the official surveyor of Shelter Island Park, who is reported to have accepted land in lieu of cash for his professional services. The other was commissioned by Bateman's sister Mrs. Cartwright.[15]

At this juncture, Motley and Pond seem to have decided to acelérate matters by building and furnishing a series of cottages for rental or sale. It is not entirely clear whether they acted in behalf of the Association, or whether they formed a quasi-private development partnership, hoping to benefit both the hotel and themselves. It will be recalled that they had already bought up dozens of unimproved lots from absentee owners who seemed eager to unload.

The first such cottage went up directly across the street from Motley's own, probably in 1886 and probably as a rental cottage; but if so, it was soon sold to a private owner. Then came triplets—three new cottages "near the Manhanset House"—the only record of which consists of a short news item in 1887 stating that plumbing was being installed in them. It is not too far-fetched to identify this trio, like the first three, from their almost identical design (especially the chimneys!) and from certain preparatory real estate transactions.[16] Two of these houses soon found a buyers, the first for $6,500 in 1889 and the second for $8,000 by 1891.

Nearly three years later there is newspaper reference to more cottages under construction by the firm of Washburne & Beale of Brockton, Massachusetts. Two of them were commissioned by Messrs. Motley and Pond, and the third— "a large one with all modern improvements, north of the Motley cottage"—by Lorenzo Woodhouse of Chicago for his daughter Grace,[17] who died three years

---

may have been his son or possibly a nephew. If so, the reference in Mayor Poor's historical essay should have been to Virgil S. rather than Virgil C. Pond.

later. The house was returned to her father by her will. Her husband was Robert B. Roosevelt, an uncle of Theodore Roosevelt and a prominent citizen of New York City; his name, prefaced by "the Honorable", is inscribed in a bronze plaque on the Brooklyn Bridge as a member of the commission which was responsible for erecting that famous span.

Of the remaining two cottages, one served the hotel as a rental guest house for many years[18], whereas the other may be identified as one that Motley and Pond sold in 1890 for $7,000 to Benjamin Atha. The purchaser was a Newark banker who, as we shall see, was to play a role second only to that of Charles Lane Poor in the ensuing two decades. The first of the houses Atha owned was torn down in 1907 to make way for a much larger place which was destined to furnish the community with one of its most spectacular fires.

Between 1883 and 1889, according to a Manhanset brochure, the number of guest cottages jumped from five to twelve. How many of them actually belonged to the hotel? No more than two or three. It seems likely that nearly every house in the small community was included in the rental category, on the reasonable assumption that most of them were available at least for part of the season—for a consideration.

Despite these recent additions, Manhanset still lagged far behind Prospect in surrounding itself with attractive cottages, whether for rent or for private use. With the exception of the cottage built for Mr. Woodhouse of Chicago, the period of private construction by people not directly involved in the hotel still lay ahead. The personal interests of Motley, Pond and Wood were so closely linked with the corporation as to be practically indistinguishable.

The question persists: why were so few cottages erected? One clue leads to the tentative conclusion that the absentee "Boston people" were largely land speculators, whereas the "Brooklyn people" bought lots with the intention of building summer homes for themselves. Maybe, as Poor believed, restrictive stipulations discouraged independent ownership near the Manhanset House. Shoreland was not for sale and all utilities belonged to the hotel. It is possible, but hardly probable, that uncongenial building restrictions placed upon lot owners may have played an inhibiting role. The following stern stipulations—inspired no doubt by vivid recollections of the "fish factories"—were carefully written into most of the early deeds:

> But neither the party of the first part nor her heirs and assigns shall or will at any time hereafter erect or permit upon any part of the land conveyed by the present Indenture, any slaughter-houses, smith shop, forge, furnace, steam engine, brass foundry, nail or other iron foundry, or any manufactory of guns, powder, glue, varnish, vitrol, ink or turpentine or for the tanning, dressing and preparing hides, skins or leather, or any ale house, brewery, distillery or other place for the manufacture or compounding of intoxicating

liquors, or for selling or dispensing the same in any form, or for the preparation, storage or deposit of manure or other fertilizing substance of offensive character, or for carrying on any other noxious, dangerous or offensive trade or business, or any building of the character or description known as a tenement house or any barn or stable...*[19]

The prohibition against barns and stables sprang, of course, from a taboo against keeping horses and rigs within sight and smell of the cottages. Aside from aesthetic and sanitary considerations, horse stables were a luxury rather than a necessity—for pleasure driving rather than convenience. Fresh meat, milk and vegetables were delivered to the cottages' back doors by local merchants or farmers with wagons. The already well-established butcher, Caleb Dawson, was confronted in 1886 with a competitor selling prime ribs for 10 cents a pound! Furthermore, opportunities for pleasure driving on the Island's public roads were limited. Summer visitors who insisted on having their own conveyances had either to rent space in a public livery or to maintain a stable on the perimeter of the community.[20]

Three of the privately owned carriage houses are still extant, though only one is readily recognizable as such. All have been converted into dwellings. The two oldest ones—probably erected about 1890—stand together on South Street close to Julia Havens' Creek. The third is completely outside the Village, beyond Gardiner Creek bridge at the foot of Winthrop Road.[21]

For "Spoiled Children of Fortune"

According to the chatty accounts of anonymous contributors to Long Island weekly papers, life at Manhanset (where apparently the term Shelter Island Park slowly lost currency) was very much in the family style, but affluently so. The 1882 promotional leaflet pointed out with pride that Manhanset management was in the hands of two men who in winter operated the gilt-edged Sherwood on Fifth Avenue at 44th Street, New York City's "largest exclusively family hotel." Since the guests of that hotel all departed in the summer, the whole staff was simply transferred to Shelter Island!

The Manhanset accommodations are designed, we are then told, to provide "comforts which are necessities to spoiled children of fortune." Such overblown prose is of course typical of the era, keeping in mind that the "comforts" included not only 800 linear feet of piazza space but also a meager number of "family-style" bathrooms for nearly three hundred guests. Plans to ameliorate this latter situation almost foundered when sixteen plumbers struck for higher wages, a couple of weeks before the opening of the 1886 season![22] It redounds to the management's credit, however, that electric light at least in the public rooms arrived as early as 1884—admittedly "a great improvement over gas." Manhanset House thus had a four-year jump on Prospect. Light standards erected at the same time in front of two of the cottages were praised as giving "a very beautiful appearance during the evening."[23]

Whether a whole summer at Manhanset could be described as exciting poses an entirely different sort of question, but by the end of the 1884 season 15,000 guests had been "entertained": "The success of the House has been almost phenomenal."[24] There were times—Fourth of July weekends, for example—when cots had to be set up to accommodate an overflow of guests.[25] For children, "straw" rides followed by ice cream treats and footraces with prizes are always exciting, notably when a team of horses happened to bolt, and dislocated both shoulders of the driver. Fortunately, no children happened to be aboard.[26] To a later generation of adults accustomed to bikinis the very thought of bathing fully clad may seem hopelessly tame, but surely not the spectacle of a harbor full of 60-foot sailers and an occasional oceangoing steam yacht such as J. P. Morgan's *Corsair* or J. Rogers Maxwell's *Celt*. In 1883 a reporter standing atop White Hill counted "165 yachts, boats and sailing craft of all descriptions".[27]

In 1886 the Shelter Island Yacht Club came into being. Frequent regattas and races across the harbor, measuring a mile and a quarter from boathouse to boathouse, evoked a natural exhilaration heightened by a strong feeling of rivalry. Concealed within the competition, of course, was the old tug of war between Boston (now being superseded by Manhattan) on the one hand and Brooklyn on the other.

For the surf-caster there were seasons when sharks five to six feet long could be landed near Dinah's Rock, within sight of the hotel veranda—and within sight of the hundreds of excursionists aboard the sidewheeling day steamers that frequently tied up there for a picnic.

During the 1880s baseball was coming into its own as the national pastime and the two hotels quickly followed the trend. "Base-Ball," it was promised, "will receive some attention this season; we have a nine here that will meet all comers[28]—this in addition to "concerts, readings, hops, croquet, archery and tennis." The challenge of the diamond was accepted not only by Prospect players but by teams as far away as Mattituck—and, to its credit, the home team more than held its own, by margins as narrow as 7-6 or as wide as 38-8. Whether these triumphs were due primarily to the skill of the guests or of the waiters remains unclear. But democracy prevailed; a commentator who noticed, during one season, that the complexions of the dining room staff had become "several shades darker," quickly added, "But some of them can play ball."

As for the other vigorous games, tennis was played gracefully on rough grass courts; the advent of golf was still a decade away. On rainy days the physical exercise of muscular Christians was pretty well confined to billiards and bowling. This is where the new Amusement Hall entered the picture, in time for the 1884 season. Erected at the rear of the hotel, probably adjacent to the tennis courts whose dim contours are still barely discernible across the road from Eastgate, it offered bowling and a variety of other indoor games for "healthy exercise."[29] However, it contributed nothing to the well-being of boss-contractor Jetter from Riverhead, who unluckily fell from its roof and broke his leg.

The previous hall, which had contained bowling alleys, was converted into a set of apartments "especially adapted for families" and dubbed The Four Cottages. A contemporary editorial observes that the new rooms will be "handsomely furnished, well ventilated and very homelike." He goes on to say, "The embankment will be made to correspond to that of the hotel and a new concrete walk will lead from the wharf to the main entrance on the front."[30] These comments may be deduced to refer to the rather low building that appears in some of the earliest photographs and prints. Later, to make room for the much larger annex of 1893, it was moved farther east.

Clams, Claret and Champagne

Evening diversions? It must be remembered that this was an era of literary and musical pretensions. While those who really enjoyed such cultural amenities reveled in them, those not so inclined a lid only suffer in silence. Professional actors and itinerant musicians found their way to the various resorts of eastern Long Island, where—in the absence of movies, radio and television—a warm welcome usually awaited them. But no one felt utterly dependent upon the arrival of traveling artists. A volunteer committee, brimful of energy, would round up "guests of the house, assisted by the orchestra" to offer weekly programs of readings and recitations interspersed with musical selections. One such midsummer event listed nineteen numbers from Overture to Finale, presented entirely by young people—including "Three Graces," consisting of as many maidens, and "Three Disgraces," an equal number of boys.

By good fortune an almost complete set of little, neatly printed programs for the 1884 and 1886 seasons was preserved in the family of Dr. Fowler, to provide a refreshing insight into the nature of those entertainments. Long accounts of the amateur performances also appeared in the *Suffolk Weekly Times*, The jovial physician not only was a regular participant in the Friday night parties but took many dry-plate photographs, now the only pictures of the colony at that time. Some of these were so successful that they reappeared year after year, without attribution, in the hotel's enticing brochures.[31]

The programs of the older generation, in contrast to the humors of youth, were usually serious and relentlessly sentimental. A mixed quartet would sing "Oh, Hush Thee My Baby," whereupon Dr. Fowler would read "Saved from the Storm." Or a solo, "Thou'rt Like a Flower," would be followed by Dr. Fowler reading "Our Jack's Come Home Today." "Living Tableaux" were always popular. One reviewer reported that "Miss Wilson looked as much like a lifeless piece of marble—Galatea—as anyone could."[32] One August evening was devoted to "Mrs. Jarley and Her Waxworks"—a popular pastime inspired by Charles Dickens' novel, *The Old Curiosity Shop*—with some remarkable impersonations of famous and infamous people, including such "figgers" as Little Nell, a two-headed girl, a Chinese giant and a Maid of Athens with Lord Byron. A week later a Minstrel Concert was presented by the "fine corps" of waiters, "modest in action, respectable in appearance," whose regular earnings amounted to $20 to $25 per month plus meals and tips which averaged $1 to $1.50 per day.

Saturday nights were given over to dancing. The dance card—if August 1, 1885 is a fair example—consisted alternately of waltzes and "Lanciers," with a March at the start, a Gavotte in the middle and a Galop at the end. Partners were reserved in advance and each name carefully inscribed opposite the contracted dance. Full-dress "Germans" with "numerous and costly" favors, the music consisting entirely of waltzes by Strauss and Waldteufel, were apparently very popular.

Clambakes were perennial favorites and some were especially memorable—such as the excursion to Rose's Grove to feast on clams, claret and champagne. On the way home those particular three C's proved to be no match for the high seas, according to the local reporter, and some picnickers "were persuaded" to contribute the one to the other.

Then, too, famous personages were constantly being drawn to the Manor House, by the hospitality of Professor and Mrs. Horsford. In one week these guests included Chief Justice C. P. Daly of New York and his family, followed by "Mrs. ex-President Tyler," who of course was Julia Gardiner of Gardiner's Island, and her family.[33] Other visitors included Sir William and Lady Thompson, he being "the greatest philosopher in all Britain."[34] This is only a sampling but leads one to assume that the summer road to and from Manhanset was fairly well traveled, if only to enjoy the view from its piazza. As a matter of fact, Sylvester Manor seems to have acquired its name about this time. A long and laudatory tribute to Professor Horsford in the *Suffolk Weekly Times* contains these intriguing words: "As his home was constituted a Manor by grant of Charles II in 1666, as Nathaniel Sylvester was once Lord of the Manor and as it has been in the possession of his posterity until the present time, it is to be known hereafter as Sylvester Manor."[35]

Then as now, sudden events had a way of intruding themselves and providing an unscheduled flutter of excitement. Sometimes these were of national significance, as in 1885, when President Grant's death drew six hundred people into Manhanset grove for a solemn memorial service. At other times, forces from the outside world rudely disrupted the hotel's peaceful life—as when the Manhanset waiters, led by a Socialist agitator, unprecedentedly went out on strike in 1882. There was a free-for-all in the grove, but the ringleaders were soon fired and tranquility restored. (One might ask whether Socialism also was responsible for the local boy who went on strike against carrying the mail back and forth to Greenport for nineteen cents per day.) A different sort of stir was caused when General William Tecumseh Sherman and his two "accomplished socialite" (not to be confused with socialist!) daughters docked their yacht to enjoy the famous hotel's hospitality for a few hours before proceeding to New England.

The Island's new life as a summer resort was thus a composite of light and dark, sweet and sour. A general balancing of the books—with due apologies for mixed metaphors—at the end of the first full decade reveals much on the credit side of the ledger but a few items on the debit side as well.

For one thing, it was observed that attendance of year-round residents at the widely advertised Temperance meetings was poor, and still declining. The weekly columnist publicly chided his fellow citizens for their delinquency: "We have often asked what has become of Temperance on our Island. Suffolk County did not use to boast of any greener spot among its temperance fields than Shelter Island, but today the light seems to be burning low." He mixed his metaphors too!

An equally plaintive note was sounded by a summer visitor at the end of the season: "There are many yachtsmen still hovering about the place but whether they are detained wholly on account of Deering Bay or partially on account of the beauty of the dear girls is a matter to be decided by themselves. But while they linger and the girls linger the Manhanset will hold her own against storm and tide, and smile in the teeth of the elements."[36] These were evidently the same girls whom another reporter would glowingly describe as "sunburnt and rugged-looking."[37]

If these statements sound like a well-rehearsed antiphon, what can be said of the image of the two hotels in the *New York Tribune*, whose reporter seems only to have rephrased in 1890 the observations he or his colleague first recorded in 1883: "Daily life is two-fold. Over at Manhanset, on the bluff, swelldom reigns. All is elegant and precise. There are a few cottages scattered irregularly about the park, but hotelism is paramount and absorbing. On the Heights, across Dering's Harbor, where the yachts lie, is jollity, life and the cottages. It is a second Brooklyn..."[38]

Shelter Island had obviously become a state of mind. It could be reached by ferry from Greenport for ten cents per person, or fifty cents per horse, mule or pleasure carriage.

Chapter IV

THE LEGENDARY NINETIES 1890-1900

SHELTER ISLAND entered the final decade of the nineteenth century with a strong prospect of becoming a leading American resort, only to be hit by the general panic of 1893 and then by two devastating fires in less than two years.

At the beginning of this period Manhanset House advertised three hundred rooms and twelve cottages available for rental. New extensions and enlargements of the hotel were sprouting in all directions, and there were plans to double its capacity. The dining room had already been widened by "twelve feet on each side for the whole length of seventy-six feet" making it "one of the largest and finest rooms used for such purpose in any summer hotel on the Atlantic coast."[1] And in 1890 a sizable white frame chapel was placed sedately on the hill behind the hotel, not unlike its cedar-shingled counterpart in the grove behind the Prospect House.

Facts about the early history of these two churches are hard to come by. For the Manhanset Chapel, whose subsequent removal will be described later, they are derived almost entirely from a few brief news items, one of which labels the little church "unique," ostensibly because it was incorporated "as a free church with no denominational allegiance." "Sittings" were gratis at a time when most churches were financed by annual pew rents. "It owes nothing and has neither endowments or regular income..."[2] Voluntary subscriptions toward building the chapel were being collected at least two years earlier. The actual construction was entrusted to Washburne, Beale & Co., the same Massachusetts firm that had built the more recent cottages. The tower contained a bell that was reported to weigh 200 pounds more than the one in the Presbyterian belfry.[3]

Services were held every Sunday morning at 11 o'clock, "the preacher being whomsoever the trustees may select for the day." Unique? Probably no more so than the Prospect Chapel, the tip of whose steeple could be seen rising above the trees across the harbor. From today's point of view the unique thing about the Manhanset church would appear to be its almost impenetrable anonymity. Except for the names of the trustees in 1900, everything about this little institution remains virtually nameless. Some of the ministers who preached in the hotel parlor before the chapel was built are mentioned briefly in news columns of the day, but the only chapel speakers—throughout the entire twenty-two year period—whose names come down to us are three men from Newark, Washington and Boston who occupied the pulpit in August 1897.

All in all, the first years of the so-called Gay Nineties were auspicious for Manhanset—especially 1892. In that year a complete reorganization took place, even more thorough than in 1879. Many of the same men were involved under the presidency of Thomas Wood, a man of small stature but considerable energy, with a big wart on his chin. A new company, the Manhanset Improvement Corporation, was formed and capitalized at $108,000. It took full control of everything-the hotel, the Shelter Island Park operation and all the real estate that Motley and Pond had meanwhile accumulated, including a dozen lots purchased from Thomas Wood. In fact Motley and Pond appear to have seized the initiative from Wood. The name of the hotel was unchanged but Shelter Island Park became Manhanset Manor, and the whole enterprise was imbued with fresh vigor. New capital, in the form of a substantial loan from the Knickerbocker Trust Company of New York was obtained in order to put up a large annex, dig new wells, provide a pumphouse and extend the electric lighting.[4]

Some idea of the upbeat mood of these years emerges from the ambitious plans for the 1893 annex. To begin with, the existing annex, which had once contained the bowling alleys, was moved 140 feet farther to the eastward from the main building. A new structure—190 feet long and four stories high—now went up between the two older buildings. To connect the new annex with the hotel proper, without interfering with traffic to and from the wharf, a "bridge" was thrown across the road. The same bridge enclosed a commodious hall designed for entertainment of all kinds—concerts, plays and balls. On rainy days it served admirably as a sheltered vantage point from which to watch the ferries come and go. The high morale of the carpenters on this project expressed itself in 200-yard "running matches" in which the first prize was a high silk hat and the second a "nice" cake.[5]

The addition of the new wing was heralded by a barrage of 25,000 promotional brochures detailing the glories of the Manhanset House, which could now accommodate six hundred guests on the American Plan, at $4 and up per day or $25 per week. The task of placing these twenty-page booklets in the mail devolved upon Georgia Lester, the young postmistress of Manhanset Manor, whose deft hand, in addition to tapping out telegraph messages, was capable of addressing five hundred envelopes in a day. The hotel thus kept in very close touch with the world, and the world reciprocated.

A page of the brochure was devoted to travel recommendations. These included the Shelter Island Special Express, leaving Long Island City at 3 P.M. every weekday afternoon, arriving at Greenport at 5:15, not counting the rides on the 34th Street ferry at one end and on the *Menantic* shuttle ferry at the other. Or one could enjoy a "delightful sail through Long Island Sound by daylight" on the "new and elegant iron steamers"—*Montauk* and *Shelter Island*—departing New York daily except Sundays at 2 P.M., touching Manhanset that evening. Bostonians could take the steamers *Manhanset* or *Long Island*, which left New London daily at 9:25 A.M., reached Greenport by 11:50, stopped at Shelter Island at noon and docked in Sag Harbor at 1 P.M. The return trip was executed with similar dispatch and dependability. The fare was one dollar.

The hotel had good reason to commend itself in glowing terms to its elite guests. Every room could communicate with the front office by bell and speaking tube. The building could be "thoroughly warmed by steam heat." "Precautions against fire are extraordinarily complete and extensive"—a claim that rings hollow in view of what was to happen only three years later. Not only was a prominent New York physician a guest-resident, but the hotel proudly promised "the joy of salt water sailing without risk of seasickness."

Stanford White Comes to Little Germany

The new corporation now turned to the task of developing the remaining 170 acres of unimproved land at Locust Point, and for the first time the names of individual cottage owners began to appear in the Town's tax lists. The size of the little colony had already doubled, starting with Motley's own house in 1883 and—thanks to the initiative of Motley and Pond—rising to a minor crescendo in 1887 and 1889. Thomas Wood, fittingly enough, opened the new decade by ordering a cottage "for his own use" from John Beale.[6] One reason for Beale's success as a building contractor during those years may have been the marvelous dexterity of one workman, who could install 2000 laths per day as compared with an average output of 800. The house Wood had previously occupied was to be moved "near the bowling alley and remodelled into a drugstore." The original site of the old house is unknown, but the drugstore stood between Eastgate and the present Village Hall.

The momentum of building continued as a different breed of builder-owner finally arrived on the scene—people who were not personally involved in the affairs of the corporation. John Lidgerwood was the first such buyer to select a lot, in virgin territory east of the hotel toward Dinah's Rock. He was known for his terrible temper, which suffered a volcanic eruption one day on the Long Island Railroad when the soft-shell crabs that he was bringing out from the city escaped from their basket and scattered in all directions.

Until Lidgerwood made his purchase of land on the Greenport Channel side, all cottages had either lined the two main residential streets leading to the bathing beach or fronted the harbor. He was quickly followed by a trio of men from Manhattan, who paid out $10,000 for three adjacent parcels on the high ground just behind his property. One of them, an architect by the name of William Schickel, designed three Victorian cottages for himself and his two friends. As all three families were both large and affluent, the resultant cottages were correspondingly capacious and impressive—not nearly so big as the hotel but distinctly larger than any previously built cottage. Subsequently these good neighbors—still in concert—enlarged their lots toward the channel and put up an elegant bathhouse with a common dock—a tripartite accommodation that persists today.

The architect was a devout Roman Catholic who later designed Our Lady of the Isle Church in the Heights. Two of his four daughters became nuns. On at least one occasion he had the distinction of entertaining the Archbishop of New York and his entourage for a weekend. Flanking his new home on either side were the summer homes of two partners in Kuttroff, Pickhardt and Co., dye importers. They were staunch Lutherans. The arrangement proved to be a most amicable and durable one. Within another year Adolph Schwarzmann, publisher of *Puck* magazine, commissioned the noted architect, Stanford White, to design a house on the bluff between Pickhardt's house and the channel. About the same time John Lidgerwood closed the circle of fine new houses by building one just east of Schwarzmann and across the road from Schickel, on the land he had bought a couple of years earlier.[1]

Indeed there is doubt whether the wide avenue that runs through it now actually penetrated that circle at that time. That it existed only on paper is suggested by an official complaint, lodged years later—1907—that a tennis court between Lidgerwood and Schickel encroached on the public right of way. Lidgerwood was then constructing a boardwalk along the beach to the hotel and probably regarded a roadway as both unnecessary and undesirable. The wagon road behind the inland cottages was more than adequate for local deliveries.

As four of these five newcomers had distinctly Germanic names and evidently spoke German both fluently and frequently, their corner of Manhanset Manor was quickly dubbed Germantown, or Little Germany— and it so appears on some informal maps until World War I. The intimate neighborhood composed of the five families remained intact, and the original ownerships were unchanged, for well over thirty years. In fact, the two remaining cottages have each changed hands only three times in the eighty years of their existence.

This spate of construction between 1890 and 1895 constituted the third and most promising step in the development of Manhanset's cottage colony that had begun with the three "gingerbread" houses twenty years before. As the hotel's 1893 brochure put it, "In the park surrounding the hotel are prettily clustered 21 attractive cottages, connected with the hotel and with each other by plank and asphalt walks. Among the handsomest of these are four built this year by private parties." The pendulum had now definitely swung toward bonafide private owners who were neither involved with the hotel company nor interested in rental income. Two of the hotel's guest cottages were also sold off, thereby giving further encouragement to this healthy new trend.

The New York Yacht Club Steps Ashore

The greatest contribution to the growing glamor of Manhanset Manor was not, however, the cluster of handsome mansions in "Germantown," but an unprepossessing cabin set up on a few piles near the bathing beach. This was Station #5, established by the New York Yacht Club in 1892, the same year in which the Shelter Island Yacht Club, founded eight years earlier, undertook to build its first clubhouse on Chequit Point just across the harbor. Rivalry again?

Interest in yachts was quickening all along the North Atlantic coast but clubs were still relatively small, few and far between. Enterprising skippers of the gilt-edged New York Club felt the need of "stations"—a sort of home away from home—where members could drop anchor on longer cruises, stretch their legs, receive mail and messages, etc. Such auxiliaries already existed on Staten Island and in Brooklyn, as a matter of local convenience, but now the policy committee believed that the time had come to plant bases still further afield— or asea.

One member of that committee happened to be Major Frank T. Robinson, whose cottage overlooked the Manhanset bathing beach.[5] The fact that the hotel made a practice of obtaining daily weather reports by telegraph direct from Washington may have impressed the committee. These reports were converted into signals flown from the hotel's flagpole: a white flag for clear or fair weather, a blue flag for rain or snow and a white flag with a black square for a cold wave. As a further refinement in those pre-radio days, a black triangular pennant placed above or below the other flag proclaimed rising or falling temperatures.

The Robinsons had summered here at least as early as 1884 and were actively involved in the amateur entertainments of the hotel. The Major was noted as having "a fine voice and good figure."[2] The station itself was set up at the south end of the hotel's bathing beach, only a few steps from the Robinson porch. It consisted of a cozy room at the end of a stubby dock running parallel to the bathing pier, only 75 yards away—and was thus ideal for swimming races back and forth.[10] ° There was a custodian on regular duty under the direct supervision of a member-in-charge, who for the first two years was none other than Robinson himself.

The Major was replaced in 1894-95 by a Frank Anthony. The only clue to his identity appears to be that in 1891 Motley and Pond sold one of the hotel's guest cottages to a Henry M. Anthony for $8,000—indicating that prices had risen steeply in the five years since Robinson bought his waterfront cottage from them for only $3,250.[11] From various news items it appears that H. M. Anthony was also a very close personal friend of Manhanset House's manager, Law son.

The third and fourth consecutive members-in-charge of Station #5, namely Tarrant Putnam and Charles Lane Poor, emerge much more clearly as three-dimensional personalities. They subsequently became the first and second mayors of the Village, by which time of course the Station was closed and its clubhouse had been towed away to become the present Sag Harbor yacht clubhouse. The structure—for those who wish to compare it with old photographs—remains virtually unchanged except for a fresh coat of paint and "inside" plumbing.

Putnam, a New York lawyer, bought the Robinson cottage in 1896 and assumed oversight of the Station that same year. Not only was he treasurer of the New York Yacht Club but he made it his Manhattan residence as well. It was during the tenure of this eminently quiet and peaceful person that all the stations were placed at the disposal of the government for use during the Spanish-American War. The Dering Harbor facility became a supply station for the mosquito fleet headquartered in New York City. Nothing more is known of its wartime record. After the 1899 season Putnam relinquished supervision of the Station to Charles Lane Poor, who the year before had built a very handsome cottage along the shore road, just next door to Putnam, and thus was in a position to keep the clubhouse clearly in sight.[12] Both of these gentlemen will receive more attention as the story of the Village unfolds.

America's Third Oldest Golf Club Tees Off

Manhanset Manor's sudden burgeoning was only one aspect of Shelter Island's explosive growth at this time. The Prospect House was being enlarged by fifty rooms and a new "boulevard" wound its way up Divinity Hill, opening up 250 new cottage sites, of which thirty-five had already been sold. "The little emerald green isle" was no longer quiet in summer but reverberated to "startling noises such as steamboat whistles every five or ten minutes."[13]

Developers had already reached out to West Neck and Menantic. Then, in the same big year 1892, two notable tycoons—Artemas Ward, advertising genius and publisher of *The Philadelphia Grocer*, and F. T. Smith, the Twenty-Mule Team Borax king—each bought hundreds of acres near the South Ferry, to be turned into splendid country estates, including model farms and even a deer park. It was Artemas Ward who, as we have noted, imported whole boatloads of manure from the horse-thronged streets of New York City to an island that had vetoed the production of fertilizer in order to become a summer refuge from the city.

The irony of the situation no doubt appealed to at least one elderly man as he read of these deliveries which were reported in the weekly paper along with tea parties and church sociables—namely Professor Horsford, the initiator of the Island's resort career. He died in 1893, the year of an unusually severe financial panic but also the year in which the new double-ended, paddle-wheeled ferry, *Menantic*, large enough to carry three teams of horses or either side, went into service, a vast improvement over the antiquated *Cambria*. Ten years before, a spontaneous tribute "of esteem and gratitude" had been paid to the squire of Sylvester Manor for his outstanding role in "improving and beautifying Shelter Island Park." One commentator wrote, "It feasts one's eyes to look at the work he has done by a most liberal expenditure of skill, toil and money."[14]

Out on Locust Point the Manhanset House and the New York Yacht Club station more than held their own. Year by year the hotel introduced further improvements and refinements. By 1893 these included the previously mentioned annex and a new staff dormitory; two years later, a fine new ice house with a capacity of 1100 tons was added. The ice was cut in blocks 22 inches square by 24 inches thick and packed away in sedge grass. Sometimes the supply was harvested on Shelter Island, giving work to about twenty teams and one hundred men. Usually, however, it came by schooner from Maine and the offloading took a week.

Another major construction project that same year was altogether unforeseen. In February 1895 a fire destroyed the hotel stable and the water tank which then stood together directly east of the present Village hall. Coaches, wagons, ten sets of harness and six good horses perished in the mysterious blaze, which also consumed the elegant carriages of several cottagers. No time was lost in planning bigger and better facilities, with stalls for ninety-six horses in a central section, flanked on one side by a two-story carriage house and on the other by living quarters for coachmen. The whole complex, with new water tanks, was relocated to a less obtrusive site south of the chapel and "east of the ball grounds." If the number of horse stalls seems excessive, let it be noted that one cottager, the Reverend Dr. Moore, was building his own stable to house the seven horses he planned to bring with him that same summer.[15]

A new game—golf—was just coming into favor with Americans. Manhanset House moved swiftly toward sponsoring what is reputed to be the third oldest golf club in the nation. Late in 1895, Thomas Wood and the hotel's manager, H. D. W. Lawson, together with an unnamed golf expert, went looking for a suitable site and settled upon a section of the Horsford estate known as Woodruff Farm. By February charter memberships in the club were available at $100 per annum, and the club was incorporated that same year. A newspaper announcement noted that the game required "an attendant to carry a bag of sticks." Estimated cost: ten cents per boy.[16]

At a time when the first impromptu courses often had no more than three holes, a Scottish expert named C. A. W. Fox was brought in to lay out nine holes in the same general area as the present Gardiner's Bay course. After a longish walk or ride through the woods, players teed off from the Colonial farmhouse that served as the first clubhouse. A paragraph from a later brochure offers this eloquent account of the first golf course on Shelter Island:

> The Club House is a quaint old Colonial mansion erected about 1770, by Thomas H. Dering, Esq. for his youngest son Henry, to whom he gave the eastern half of his estate, Sylvester Manor. His ancestors took title to the property from Nathaniel Sylvester, first proprietor of Shelter Island. From these hills, in the Revolution, the people gathered to watch the British men-of-war when they were wintered in Gardiner's Bay. Here were the "Culloden," the "Royal George," the "Grand Duke," and six or seven more great ships. All the timber on the north of the island was felled, and, with such grain and food as could be collected, shipped at Hay Beach Point in transports to New York. On Mount Pleasant a beacon was kindled at the close of the war, sending the tidings eastward. It has been rejuvenated and sumptuously furnished, and from the broad verandas one may look here into shadowy and romantic forest glades, there across the grassy, wind-swept downs, and yonder to the blue waters of Gardiner's Bay and the vast seas beyond.[17]

It is worth digressing to point out that General Thomas Dering was noted in his time as "an ardent Merino enthusiast," who improved his flock by importing rams from Spain when the "Merino mania" was driving up the cost to $800 per head. He had the satisfaction of supplying several yards of fine homespun "cassimere" from Shelter Island for the new suit worn by President Madison at the New Year reception in the White House in 1811.[18]

The only untoward event of that first season on the links occurred when that prominent cottager, Benjamin Atha, was knocked down by the careless swing of a young man's "stick" at the fourth (or Triangle) hole and lay unconscious for twenty-five minutes. Later Mr. Atha became in effect the patron saint of the course.

Tourneys served to increase the popularity of the game, and soon another course was laid out on what is frequently called "Goat Hill," at the southern end of the camp-meeting grounds. Mr. Fox was succeeded as golf instructor at Manhanset by a Willie Hunter who, it is said, went on to win the first British amateur championship. In those days the holes were tagged with exotic names, as though they had been Alpine peaks, rather than by simple numbers. Soon the little white ball was vying with the big white sail for the attention of summer visitors. In fact, as we shall see, it was to be golf rather than yachting that helped the Dering Harbor community to rise out of the ashes of the greatest conflagration twenty years later. Despite the interruption of two world wars and through three changes of name, the club continues to thrive as the Gardiner's Bay Country Club. But in the meantime the first of two disastrous fires had occurred, in the very year the course opened.

Manhanset House Destroyed By Flames!

About breakfast time on August 13, 1896 a small fire broke out in the laundry behind the hotel and, jumping a narrow alley, began licking at the dining room wing of the big wooden structure. At the northeast corner of the main building the flames met a light breeze and soon engulfed the main unit. Equipment was rushed from Greenport to assist the local firefighters but the available water supply proved totally inadequate. It then became a matter of preventing the enormous bonfire from devouring everything. A brief attempt to cut the bridge leading to the new annex had to be abandoned, in favor of stationing men wrapped in wet blankets on its roof to fight off the advancing flames. The roofs of several cottages were occasionally ignited by flying embers.[19]

Scores of volunteers manned the bucket brigades, working in the intense heat until many were at the point of exhaustion and collapse. When the lack of water became evident, young blades from nearby cottages even brought seltzer bottles into play! Lawson, the manager, was badly burned and lost most of the skin on his face. More than two months later a bed of live coals "enough to cook the dinner of all the housewives on Shelter Island, was discovered under the debris."[20] Meanwhile emergency measures had been promptly taken to care for the guests, who had all managed to escape with their personal effects. Many were carted—quite literally—to the Prospect House, others were dispatched by boat to New London. The annex was soon filled with those who elected to stay on and three small dining rooms were hastily improvised—also a telegraph office, in the company house where the Village hall now stands. These interim arrangements proved to be so "jolly" that some of the evacuated guests reportedly insisted on returning from New London to complete their vacations!

Morale was high, and there was no hesitation about the decision to rebuild. In October a Boston firm began clearing the site and during the winter many schooners tied up at the wharf to unload a million feet of lumber, along with tons of nails and iron girders. Work went briskly forward despite heavy snows in February, which kept seventy men with shovels busy removing armpit-high drifts from Village roads. A sensation second only to that of the fire itself was produced by the removal—by Hopping and Topping of Bridgehampton—of the great smokestack, variously estimated to contain anywhere from 38,000 to 60,000 bricks, to its new location beside the equally new laundry, as extra insurance against future fires.[21]

According to Professor Poor, who himself was a guest in the hotel at the time of the fire, the decision to rebuild was a mistake.[22] The addition of a dining room and kitchen to the surviving annexes would, in his judgment, have been adequate in view of the fact that the vogue of huge summer hotels was passing. But "Mr. Wood and his associates could not change with the times." It is true that vacation patterns were shifting, as more people chose to build summer homes and others preferred to "weekend" rather than settle down for a month or more. But it was not easy in 1896 to argue against the prevailing euphoria of the still "brilliant" seasons at Shelter Island, which was believed to be "quite as gay as the French sea resorts." Indeed the hotel's continuing prosperity during the next several years culminated in the building of still another annex consisting of twenty-four rooms.[23]

Wisely or unwisely, Manhanset House stubbornly geared its policy to the concept of a family resort hotel where well-to-do people would stay for weeks and to which they would return year after year. Privately owned cottages, although actively fostered, continued to be little more than "mere adjuncts"—Poor's phrase—dependent upon the hotel for all services and held hostage to its support. They were expected to open and close when the hotel did, thereby limiting their out-of-season usefulness. The company still refused to sell any land abutting the beaches—a policy which in itself seems to have been an enlightened one.

By the following summer a new main structure was open for business. There were conflicting views regarding it. One reporter described it favorably enough yet in words that were somewhat ambiguous. The new unit, he wrote, "has none of the things which it ought not to have... no inferior rooms... the ground floor entirely public... including women's billiard parlors."[24] But Professor Poor's opinion was decidedly unfavorable. "The new building was huge, but unattractive and not very substantial." The small generator was "sufficient only to light the main floor and public rooms." Everything else—bedrooms and cottages-operated on acetylene gas. According to him, the hotel, poorly furnished and heavily in debt, "was unsuccessful from the day it reopened."

There is undoubtedly some truth in Poor's estimate of the situation, especially with respect to the heavy burden of indebtedness that hung over the enterprise, but also regarding the irksome limitations laid upon the cottages. Before and after the season many owners had to stay in local boarding houses when they visited the Island. Nevertheless the general outlook must have seemed fairly bright, as the hotel's patronage gave every indication of holding steady, and even improving. Shelter Island, with Deauville and Newport in mind, was in no mood to be discouraged, even by the fires which in a short decade had also leveled "a store, a post-office, a telegraph office, a public library and a church."[25] And wood remained the most common building material.

Bubble, Bath, Bubble

Two more cottages sprang up in the wake of the great conflagration of 1896, joining the parade along the shore of Dering Harbor toward Julia Havens' Creek instead of eastward toward Little Germany. The new owners happened to be predominately of Scottish or English origin, with Professor Poor taking the lead.

His first cottage, as already indicated, occupied a choice spot across from the New York Yacht Club station. Designed by Rossiter and Wright of New York, it appears from photographs to have been a very impressive three-story house with a lofty Colonial veranda. With its valuable heirlooms and fine antiques the house was assessed at $25,000. It was called Laneholm for an infant son, Charles Lane Poor, Jr., and a maternal grandfather.

Another house erected along the harbor shore at that time calls for special recognition, both because it remains virtually unchanged and because of an improbable association.[26] Oral tradition has it that this substantial cottage was built as a hideaway for the well-known actress, Minnie Maddern Fiske, by a "benefactor" and that she—or they—came out from New York by private yacht. As would befit a star of the stage, it has a large bathroom with elaborate fixtures and colorful tiles adorned with cupids and flowery garlands—the only one of its kind in Manhanset Manor, but Mrs. Fiske's connection with it has not been established.

The prosaic truth seems to be that in 1900 a John N. Luning, prominent member of the New York Yacht Club, bought seven lots from the Manhanset Improvement Corporation and declared his intention to invest $30,000 in a cottage for himself.[27] Two years later he was assessed at $25,000 and for years, beginning in 1906, he was to be, along with Professor Poor, one of the very few Manhanset Manorites listed as legal residents of Shelter Island. As for a relationship, if any, between Mr. Luning and Mrs. Fiske, there is nothing to suggest even a casual acquaintance. Nor is there any evidence to suggest that she ever rented the cottage from him or through some agent. And, if there were, subsequent rental could hardly explain the very elaborate bathroom.

Careful scrutiny of Mrs. Fiske's biography[28] affords no inkling of any "benefactor," nor any hint that she ever visited Shelter Island. Wistfully assuming nevertheless that the actress *may* have occupied the cottage, it can only be said that Dering Harbor had no reason to deprecate her presence. Born in New Orleans around the close of the Civil War, she made a precocious stage debut at the age of two, became a star of the New York stage at sixteen, married a prominent theatrical editor and publisher, and went from triumph to triumph as a dramatic actress. She introduced Henrik Ibsen's controversial heroines to the U. S. public, beginning with *A Doll's House* in 1894, played Becky Sharp for years, fought at great personal sacrifice to break a tyrannous theatrical trust—and appears to have led a thoroughly exemplary family life. This account stands in stark contrast to that of another celebrated stage personality who a decade later did unquestionably occupy a cottage nearby.

With or without Mrs. Fiske, Shelter Island and Manhanset Manor at the turn of the century both had every reason to think big. Their renown was more widespread before World War I than it was to be after World War II, by which time Prospect House too had fallen victim to the flames. Feature articles on the Island appeared in the metropolitan dailies of Brooklyn, Manhattan and Boston. Issue after issue of the *Suffolk Weekly Times*, published in Greenport, gave it front-page coverage. It, as well as other papers in nearby Southold, Sag Harbor and elsewhere enlisted "stringers" who sent in long dispatches full of names and local details. One obviously enraptured correspondent interrupted his monotonous listing of hotel guests to exclaim, "Shelter Island in all her former glory never approached the splendor of 1899. Never before have summer visitors flocked to her shores in such almost countless numbers as they have this season... The rush is on for bathhouses... all those long rows of houses are unable to supply the demand... "[29] Considering that the Prospect House alone had about 250 bathing cabins where the Beach Club now stands, the superlatives can hardly be called exaggerated.

The same writer, in describing a regatta at the Yacht Club, marvels at the large numbers of "handsome equipages" coming up to the turnstile entrance to the clubhouse grounds on Chequit Point. He concludes by calling the Island a "young Newport." Naturally there were some world-weary guests who refused to be carried away, such as the one at Manhanset House who remarked in the hearing of a *New York Tribune* reporter, "If you like to do nothing better than anything else, Shelter Island's the place to come to."

Wheels Require Roads

To be sure, the Island still had a few bumps. The condition of its roads, for instance! Metaphorically speaking, the way into the twentieth century was rough and getting rougher. In the interests of both business and pleasure— which was also good business—something had to be done. With traffic on the increase, every spell of bad weather seemed to make matters worse. Large boats sometimes lay idle at Manhanset wharf for days on end waiting for wagons loaded with farm produce that could not get through the deep mud. The Heights superintendent tried covering his roads with alternate layers of beach gravel and loam—which apparently helped only a little. In summer, complaints grew louder as the livery business suffered owing to "dirty roads."

Poor roads had been more or less taken for granted until the advent of the bicycle on eastern Long Island about 1893, when suddenly this new means of locomotion became the rage.[30] That was also the year of the Columbian Exposition at Chicago, memorable not only for its glorification of science but also for its frivolous Midway featuring ferris wheels and the gyrations of Little Egypt. Needless to say, many Islanders briefly abandoned Peconic Bay for the shores of Lake Michigan that summer. Perhaps they brought the bicycle virus back with them.

With "wheelmen" in the lead, pressure for better roads increased. The Town's road commission was accused of simply pushing pulverized dirt back toward the center of the roadway. The biggest improvement in years seems to have been the construction of a wider bridge over Gardiner Creek— Manhanset's front door, so to speak—so that two teams could pass abreast. By 1895, an assembly of "wheelmen, horsemen and pedestrians" (note the order of priority!) formed a club to promote better roads and, as a by-product, better relations with off-Island cyclists. It was pointed out that cyclists too were taxpayers and deserved consideration by the road commissioners. After all, a wheel cost as much as $200, in a day when a man's suit cost less than $20. As long-distance cycling—to and from Orient, Riverhead or the Hamptons for instance—became commonplace, there was agitation for a network of special side paths throughout eastern Long Island. The various makes and weights of bicycles preempted a leading place in conversation and in the writing of gossip columns. Attention was called to the fact that Dr. Benjamin—the Island's progressive young physician and a son-in-law of the Presbyterian minister—on his new, 19V2-pound Lowell Diamond wheel could respond to nearby emergencies "in less time than it takes to harness a horse."[31]

But these pedal-pushers were mere trailblazers in the cause of better roads. Two-wheelers soon gave pride of place to four-wheelers as the first automobiles chugged into the picture, and the whole world became road-conscious. Early notice of this new turn of events is given in a brief item about Dr. Benjamin's new Standhope Buggy, described as the "toniest in town."[32] Although he was most probably the first resident owner of an automobile, as well as one of the first cyclists, he was certainly not the first to drive one over the Island's unpaved roads. Two summer visitors vie for that honor in the contradictory annals of North Shore papers. The *Suffolk Times* credits a physician, Dr. William Butler, with introducing the horseless carriage in 1893, which seems almost too early. The *Riverhead News*, however, accords him second place after the Reverend Dr. Aspinwall, rector of St. Thomas Episcopal Church in Washington, D. C, who "forsook his steamyacht some two seasons for automobiling" when he acquired "one of the finest of self-propelled vehicles."[33] The clergyman had been sailing these waters for many years, licensed not only as captain and pilot but as chief engineer as well. He also served as chaplain of the Yacht Club.[34]

In any event, a reference dated July 14, 1900, indicates that the two gentlemen had the roads pretty much to themselves before Dr. Benjamin's Standhope Buggy joined them: "Two automobiles may be seen daily on our streets, and as yet no accident has happened. We think people are unduly scared at this innovation, when the auto is guided by careful men like Drs. Aspinwall and Butler."[35] One week later, the reporter had to eat his words. The "first runaway of the season" had occurred when an auto frightened the tethered horse of a Singer Sewing Machine agent. The animal bolted from the center of town toward Manhanset but was soon halted without injury or damage to anyone. For once no names were mentioned, but the so-called "problem" of the woman driver was looming on the horizon! "This season Mr. Elihu Frost of New York will make the third member. Mrs. Frost was one of the first automobilists in Washington, D. C. Last season her automobiling was one of the features of Newport life."[36]

Viewed rationally, the difference between 1899 and 1900 should be no greater than the difference between any other two adjacent years but, in effect, one remarkable century was closing and another, symbolized by the horseless carriage, was commencing. The restraints (often artificially imposed) and the standards (frequently double) of the Victorian era were coming under heavy attack. Summer resorts lay along the front line of attack.

Progress Is a Two-pound Oyster

The question of temperance, for example, had been publicly debated for many decades. Societies were formed, campaigns mounted, counterattacks launched—with newspapers eagerly reporting each thrust and parry. In 1898 and again in 1900 the licensing of liquor sales came to a vote on Shelter Island, where the Columbian Temperance Society, founded in 1842, had been aggressively, some said intemperately, active. Prohibition forces had a stout champion in the Presbyterian minister who, along with his deacons, also strongly denounced the dancing that followed a fireman's banquet.[37] The outcome of the vote on licensing was, so to speak, a clearcut compromise. The majority voted *against* licensing saloons, general stores and drugstores but *in favor of* licensing the hotels. The Islanders were not to be unduly subject to temptation, but neither was the resort business to be unduly handicapped. The same consideration prevailed when it was decided to distribute mail on Sundays—until so many hackles appear to have been raised that Sunday deliveries were quietly abandoned.

The world and Shelter Island were coming closer together with every passing season. It—the world, that is—still looked to many Islanders very much like the oyster that was found by a clamdigger in Chase's Creek. The enormous bivalve weighed two pounds and measured more than nine by five inches. Its publicity value was enormous—but could the monster safely be swallowed? What good was it except as a curiosity? With tons of succulent Long Island oysters now being eagerly consumed in Britain and around the globe, the guarded reaction of one local oracle was to ask, "Is it any wonder so many foreigners want all our land under water for oyster culture?" The bivalved question, still unanswered as the century ended, was plainly whether the world would be Shelter Island's oyster or Shelter Island the world's oyster.

Chapter V

A CONCLUSIVE
CONFLAGRATION
1900-1910

IN RETROSPECT the opening decade of the twentieth century at first looks curiously uneventful for Shelter Island, or at least for Manhanset Manor. These Edwardian years have sometimes been called the Naughty Aughties, probably in an effort to prolong the nostalgic image of the Gay Nineties. Despite the dalliance that was undoubtedly indulged, even at Manhanset Manor, as we shall see, the prevailing social atmosphere was one of affluent innocence—a belief in the ultimate perfectibility of man as proclaimed in the philosophy of Herbert Spencer, a pillar-of-society posture as reflected in the portraits of John Singer Sargent. In America it was, at least at the seashore, an era of prosperous propriety, during which their Imperial Majesties in Great Britain, Germany and Russia commanded an awe bordering on vicarious allegiance. No one in his right twentieth century American mind dreamed of future holocausts.

Glossy brochures of the Manhanset House continued to paint an idyllic picture, hardly altering the romantic text from year to year or updating the scenic views. The Spanish-American War had come and gone without visible impact, even though Dr. Fowler, still the resident physician of the hotel as well as a staunch member of the Union League Club of New York City, was known to have gone to Havana to organize a hospital system for the U. S. Army.

At its end, each successive summer was declared to have been "the best season in history." The new century opened on a note of financial optimism with the Manhanset House happily revealing that the month of July 1901 had seen the largest month's business in its history.[1] Two years later, Shelter Island as a whole still glowed with healthy prosperity: "There is great activity among carpenters, painters, masons and all laborers, so much that it is difficult to get a man... The full dinner pail is a familiar object here and with few exceptions our people will be wise enough to vote for continued good times by supporting the Republican ticket." It was estimated that $100,000 worth of work was being done.[2]

The year 1906 offered more of the same. An extension had been added to Manhanset's "automobile house." On July 28 the dining room had served more than 550 paying customers. Golf was more popular than ever, now that the number of holes had been increased from 9 to 19 (*sic*), covering three and a quarter miles.[3] Baseball retained its all-American allure, and the inter-hotel rivalry was as keen as ever. This was the year when John Philip Sousa, the March King himself, *pitched* for the Manhanset nine! That he also raised a baton to lead the hotel orchestra is an unfounded rumor but that he swung a bat is hard fact in the history of the hotel. It is likewise recorded that Sousa and his wife during their stay presided over a *"genuine* clambake" at Paradise Point.

Behind the Facade—Debts and Dalliance

In looking back on this era, Charles Lane Poor found an ugly worm at the core of the apple. "The hotel register of the early nineties had contained the names of many prominent families of New York and New England... [Now] the company was forced to lower its standards and to take as guests everyone who could pay... Managers were changed, prices were lowered... The prestige of Manhanset had been lost... The day of the large summer hotel was gone... The coming of the automobile and motor boat greatly accelerated the change and turned the summer hotel into a glorified tourist's camp."[4]

Professor Poor's narrative does not spell out his standard of social acceptability. Did it or did it not, for example, include Sousa or Mayor Carter H. Harrison of Chicago—or Mrs. Leslie Carter, one of the nation's most noted, and possibly notorious, ladies of the stage? In any event, the fact that she rented the Cartwright cottage—not far from the Poors'—"as heretofore," indicates that 1906 was not her first summer on the shores of Dering Harbor. The most vivid recollections of her visits focus on a swank French touring car whose uniformed chauffeur wore puttees and a waxed moustache.[5] Many years later, the house she occupied would be moved away from the road and dramatically remodeled.[6] Back of it at that time was a smaller building which David Belasco, the noted impresario, used as a studio and where he is believed to have worked on *The Girl of the Golden West*, The studio disappeared when the big house was moved but Belasco's large square piano found a permanent home in the main house.

Aside from their association with Manhanset Manor, Mrs. Carter and Minnie Maddern Fiske seem to have had only one thing in common, namely a courageous and unremitting opposition to the ruling theatrical syndicate. Eventually they helped to defeat it. Both women had outstanding success on Broadway and could defy the syndicate with impunity. Even today the vibrant Mrs. Carter is remembered for a spine-tingling performance in Belasco's *The Heart of Maryland*. In the final act, after a frantic climb to a belfry, she uttered the immortal line, "The curfew shall not ring tonight!" as she seized the wildly swinging clapper with both hands and muffled the bell's sound with her fragile body.

Mrs. Carter's arrival at Manhanset Manor in 1906 proved more sensational than usual. In July, after a courtship of only a few days, the famous star—now nearly forty-five years old—had married an "unknown" younger actor in Portsmouth, New Hampshire. They had motored to New London and chartered a tug for the voyage to Shelter Island. For all practical purposes this marked the end of her career, although she attempted many comebacks. David Belasco, her friend and mentor for fifteen years, abruptly canceled her part in his new play and refused ever to speak to her again. Later that year, when the cornerstone of the new Belasco Theater on 44th Street was laid, it was Blanche Bates, his reigning star, who doused it in champagne.

Mrs. Carter's private life had been unconventional throughout. Born Caroline Louise Dudley, at the age of eighteen she had married Leslie Carter, a wealthy Chicago industrialist. Nine years later he divorced her for adultery in what *The New York Times* called "the most indecent and revolting divorce trial ever heard in the Chicago courts." Women and boys were forbidden to attend. It was said that "she was not beautiful" but "had red hair down to her knees, one shade hotter than Titian," with a temperament to match. By then nearly thirty and totally without acting experience, she "whose momentary claim on the public's attention was anappalling notoriety" nevertheless determined on a theatrical career, beginning at the top. She prevailed upon David Belasco to become her teacher by tenaciously following him to a working hideout in the Adirondacks, where the intensity of her plea overcame his initial doubts as to her "emotional power." She was equally strong-willed in continuing to use her married name: "I hate the name; consequently I will bear it to the end. It shall hound him until his last day."[1]

A local chronicler records that Mrs. Carter was later served with a dispossess notice and sued for back rent by Miss Nancy Munro, a socialite friend whose New York apartment she had shared. The Munros, incidentally, were summer residents of Shelter Island Heights. A couple of years later the aging actress went into voluntary bankruptcy—but by that time she had plenty of company. The panic that hit the country in 1907 was more severe than anything since the time of Cleveland's election in 1893, or of Grant's election in 1873. Down went the Knickerbocker Trust Company, which had financed the Manhanset House in the 1890s.

Short-term Loans, Long-Distance Phones

Naturally the hotel's twenty-four-page prospectus, with its thirty-five photographs, gave no hint that the proprietors might have qualms about the 1907 season. Only later did it become fully apparent that fiscal termites had long been eating at the "stately pile of buildings," in which "seventy rooms heretofore not connected with private baths have been made into handsome and comfortable suites." Long-distance telephone service had been installed in every room, superseding the old system of internal bell and speaking tube. Telephone lines ran to the golf club, the bathing pavilion, the garage and stable, as well as to several of the cottages. Such up-to-date service, the brochure boasted, was "unusual in short season houses."

These major improvements were expensive and did not include unforeseen items such as the replacement of the great new water tank which incredibly caught fire, almost taking the chapel with it. The accident occurred in the early spring in the course of an effort to thaw out frozen pipes. Another misfortune had been a bolt of lightning which shattered the tall flag pole. But the loss of the tank represented a double blow to the budget, its predecessor, the old tank near the stables, having burst its hoops, "with a rush of water equal to the falls of Niagara," only the year before.

Apparently the proprietors—as personified in Thomas Wood—still reckoned that the mortgage of $80,000 on the hotel itself and $8,500 on its three cottages could safely be carried. Money, the token of success, appeared to be as plentiful as ever. After all, the trio of owners at "Germantown" had bought more land and were spending $1,400 on a commodious bathhouse and dock; and their neighbor Lidgerwood, as previously mentioned, was building a 500-foot boardwalk to the hotel. An overflow of guests at Prospect House had to sleep on cots or be farmed out. The Shelter Island Yacht Club boasted a fleet of thirty-seven steam yachts and launches, forty-one schooners, sloops and yawls, nineteen catboats and dories. And the ferry shuttled back and forth "with an auto about every trip... in fact, they are doing a two-horse business with one horse," according to the "Newsy Notes and Personals of People from the Pretty Resort Across the Bay."[8]

A year later the memory of the brief panic was already receding. Prospect House offered 276 new bathhouses and by July 4 Manhanset House illuminated Locust Grove with 16,000 lights imported from Paris, the City of Lights. Entertainment became increasingly elaborate, including grand opera and ostensibly "the world's greatest baritone" who remains nameless. To celebrate homecoming week, the management sponsored an auto race from Long Island City to Greenport.

It is worth pausing a moment to record how the hotel saw itself, in the eyes of its manager, J. Hull Davidson:

> He that once enjoys the pleasures and bounties of Shelter Island never wants to Summer elsewhere. At the eastern extremity of Long Island, it is the Mecca for automobilists and yachtsmen, and accessible by Long

Island Railroad or Montauk Boats to everybody else. An automobile party after traversing the lovely fields and shores of picturesque Long Island, with attending glimpses of beautiful landscapes and the ocean blue, find themselves at the climax of what has seemed a dream. A ferry boat similar to those that cross at Thirty-fourth Street in New York lands the automobile in five minutes after reaching Greenport on terra firma, at Shelter Island, where a commodious garage in the hands of a professional is found among the many advantages of the famous Manhanset House...

To convince one of the unsurpassed equipment of this hotel needs only a glance at the stately pile of buildings on the wooded bluff above the harbor; at the spacious and cheery office and reception hall; at the new bay-windowed dining room; at the great music room; at the luxurious suites of rooms, each with a private bath; at the ladies' billiard room; at the new fireproof kitchen, or at the group of tributary buildings a fifth of a mile away, comprising laundry, engine house, electric dynamo house and servants' quarters, all far removed from sight or sound of the hotel. Or if one would know what facilities for out-of-door delights are here afforded, he may note the attractive station of the New York Yacht Club, the well-equipped Manhanset stables, with horses and vehicles for riding and driving, commodious garage for convenience of automobilists, or the nearby links and club house of the Shelter Island Golf Club.

The grim reality behind all this rhetoric was exposed by the appointment, in December 1908, of David Simpson as trustee in bankruptcy of the Manhanset Improvement Corporation. A month later the manager himself went into bankruptcy, along with his Miami hotel and the several thousand dollars he owed Manhanset House. In the nick of time before the season opened the trustees found a new manager in the person of George F. Adams of Old Point Comfort, Virginia. He leased the hotel for five years at an annual rent of $17,500, which could, however, be reduced by 10 per cent, in the event of a ban against the sale of liquor on the Island.[2]

Hoping no doubt to restore or even enhance Manhanset's special image, the new manager opened an outdoor dining room with à la carte service and maintained a sixty-foot yacht for cruising parties. A branch of Wesley Smith's pharmacy at the Heights was set up in an old cottage—Thomas Wood's?—near the hotel.

So, on the surface the picture was rosy again, though a closer look at Shelter Island's cottage colonies would have revealed that unprecedented numbers of the large summer homes, both in the Heights and in Manhanset Manor, were being offered for rent. A prominent realtor, Ralph Duvall, had begun publishing an annual catalog with a detailed description of each rental property usually accompanied by a snapshot. By 1909 this booklet had grown about fifty pages and well over a hundred offerings, including—on the Manhanset side—not only the perennially available Cartwright and Bateman cottages but practically all of the other houses except those in "Little Germany." Renting one's cottage had evidently become preferable to occupying it—partly because European grand tours were increasingly fashionable and the additional income could cover all or a portion of the expenses.

Seasonal rents at Manhanset ranged from $600 for the Norwood cottage to $1,350 for Maplehurst and were generally higher than the cost of similar places in the Heights. The convenience of location, the quality of views, preferably waterfront, and the number of bedrooms seemed to be the determining factors. As a general rule, all households came completely furnished, down to the "stationary washtubs" which advertisements never failed to note. Certain names, too, appeared to have special drawing power: Norwood, Maplehurst, Kenwood, Fairview, Home-crest and Oaklawn.[10]

A Banquet, a Blizzard and a Ball of Fire

Thus matters stood around the proud Manhanset House in the summer of 1909. Most of the houses were being rented out and—with one exception— no more new ones were being built; but the hotel was going strong. On the weekend of July 4 the "traditional" homecoming was celebrated in a blaze of illumination with no inkling that it was destined to be the last.

A surviving menu card of the banquet that Saturday night reveals a choice of thirty-five dishes, some of which merely garnished the table. Assuming, however, that the American Plan was operative and the diner could order as much as he or she fancied, the likelihood remains that many a trencherman ate his way through several substantial courses, from caviar and/or clams to lobster à la Newburgh, followed by sweetbreads or stuffed green pepper, Philadelphia squab en casserole, a salad, Charlotte Russe parisienne, cheese and coffee—not counting a variety of vegetables, including boiled samp, and a multiplicity of desserts. What a way to go!

In 1910 the new year brought a blizzard that washed out bulkheads on both sides of Dering Harbor, "knocking everything scalawag." But plans for the ensuing season went forward—including, at last, an ice-manufacturing plant which soon stood ready for use at a cost of $20,000. No longer would there be any need to transport hundreds of tons of frozen water from Maine, or to harvest it from local ponds and store it against summer use.

Alas, to use an exclamation favored in those days, at 1:23 on the morning of May 14 a "ball of fire from over Greenport way" struck the Manhanset House a fatal blow. Mrs. Pickhardt, looking from her bedroom window not far away, at first thought that Halley's comet, observed only the evening before, had doubled back on its course. But what struck was no passing comet. The majestic complex of buildings, including the adjoining annexes, and even the freight house on the dock, went up in spectacular flames. When the caretaker tried to get to the silver closet, the halls were already full of smoke. On account of the heat it soon became impossible to approach nearer than the Chapel. In a shower of sparks the hotel's great tower tilted seaward, pitched down the bluff and struck the water with a tremendous hiss. Only the timely arrival of a soaking rain saved the nearby drugstore, the post office, one small annex and the cottage colony from incineration.

Although the hotel was not yet open for the season, its principal owner, Thomas Wood, happened to be staying at Ye Clark House, Greenport's best hotel. In the wan light of the following day he quickly reviewed the situation. In round figures the Manhanset House represented a total investment of $550,000. Its estimated value was $375,000. There was a mortgage of $135,000. Insurance coverage amounted to only $150,000.

Mr. Wood's immediate conclusion was that this time the hotel would not be rebuilt. He was old, tired and unwell. He had after all, been intimately involved with the enterprise since its inception nearly forty years before and had lived through the less disastrous fire of 1896. Now he wanted "rest and freedom from large affairs." But for others hope died hard—especially for the new manager, who held a five-year lease and an option to buy the property for $200,000. In response to inquiries, he circulated reports that a new and modern hotel would be erected immediately. Backed by a New York City bank, he laid claim to the site and to the insurance; but his assets were evidently inadequate, and the Manhanset Improvement Corporation successfully rebutted his effort.

Life would never be quite the same on Shelter Island without its flossiest hotel but the summer of 1911 arrived as usual and on schedule. Curious visitors also arrived to gape at the charred ruins and, despite posted guards, to search the ashes for retrievable mementoes. The cottages were occupied once again, the post office was moved from the hotel premises to the New York Yacht Club station and the golf course was tentatively opened for business.

Was the fire an unmitigated tragedy? According to Professor Poor, viewing the event after the passage of twenty years, "This fire was, at the time, considered a catastrophe... the Island's greatest disaster... In reality it proved to be of outstanding benefit... The hotel company was in financial difficulties, its building and its plant were in sore need of repairs... in fact, a white elephant on the hands of its owners. Had it not been destroyed it would have become more and more dilapidated... obliged to cater to less desirable elements... The surrounding cottages would have been, one by one, deserted by their owners... and the entire property... developed into the cheapest kind of a seaside resort."[11]

The Robert Roosevelt Cottage
(also The Whitney Cottage) on Locust Point, built 1890

Manhanset Chapel, now an artist's studio near Island's center. Erected 1890

N.Y. Yacht Club Station at Manhanset, 1892-1910,
now Sag Harbor Yacht Club

Poor had his own clear vision of the kind of hotelless resort to be preferred. Above all he wanted to retain the New York Yacht Club station. With that end in view, he and his wife deeded a quarter acre of shorefront to the Club after the Manhanset House burned down—which, strangely, was not adjacent to the Station but included part of the defunct hotel's bathing beach.[12] But the strategy did not succeed. The Station was discontinued and the shorefront was deeded back to Professor Poor after an interval of three years.

Cottage Owners Form Their Own Company

Meanwhile two whole years were required to bury the past, pay off old debts—e.g., to the Greenport Steam Laundry[13]—and come to grips with the future. Exactly one year after the terrible blaze the property with its remaining buildings went up for auction at the Brooklyn Real Estate Exchange[14] and was apparently sold for the "ridiculously low price" of $38,000 to a purchaser by the unfamiliar name of Walter E. Frew.[15] He quietly transferred the property to the Corn Exchange Bank to protect its mortgage. Meanwhile it was noised abroad that the sale had not been concluded; that the three best cottages would be sold off separately; and then that they had been put back into the total package. Reporters for the *Suffolk Weekly Times* faithfully reported whatever they heard, which was mostly gossip.

By midsummer, however, there was a more substantial report: that a group of Manhanset cottagers, prominent members of the New York Yacht Club, had acquired the whole 180-acre tract from the Corn Exchange Bank of New York for $85,000. The actual price seems to have been $75,000. Part of the plan was to build a Casino—that is, a private yachting and golf club—rather than another big hotel. Several resident and nonresident stockholders had indeed invested sums ranging from $500 to $7,500 in a corporation which took the name of Island Realty Company. Thus the Manhanset Improvement Corporation followed the hotel itself into oblivion. Before the year ended Thomas Wood had died in Pennsylvania, aged 82; he was buried in Massachusetts—where, in one sense, the career of Shelter Island Park had begun.

There had been compelling reasons for the property owners to band together in order to secure the assets of the old corporation. As Charles Lane Poor wrote in an unsigned statement a couple of months later, "Several cottage owners on adjacent property made the purchase to protect themselves." There were indeed whispered fears of "concessions" that might degenerate into some kind of Coney Island boardwalk. Perhaps there were lingering recollections of the circumstances that had induced Professor Horsford to close down the picnic ground at Dinah's Rock when he could no longer approve the way it was being either operated or patronized. As late as 1970 one of Shelter Island's authentic oldtimers, Charles Case, reflected the Town's vivid sentiments concerning Dinah's Rock. "I could tell you what they had in that park," declared Mr. Case. "They had a lot of drunks for one thing. Those excursion steamers used to come from Connecticut loaded with all kinds of people and plenty of liquor."[16]

A more immediate consideration however, was that all the cottages depended on essential services—water, fuel, street maintenance, sewage, etc.—heretofore provided by the hotel. In the summer following the fire, practically all these services were halted by the bank, and the direct ferry to Greenport ceased to run. This was what had really aroused the cottage owners and soon led them, via cumbersome interim arrangements, to the formal incorporation of the Village a few years later.

The prime movers of the Island Realty Company were Charles Lane Poor and Benjamin Atha. To quote once again from Professor Poor's unsigned statement circa 1916, "Mr. Poor was largely instrumental in organizing the company and in getting subscriptions for the stock. The purchase and sale agreement with the Corn Exchange Bank was signed by Benjamin Atha and C. L. Poor, who later assigned the agreement to the Island Realty Company."[17]

Both men enjoyed senior status accruing from long years of summer residence and constructive participation in the activities of the resort community. They were strong-willed men, each accustomed to having his own way—and their notion of how to do things did not always coincide. Even after the passage of three score years, the clash of their personalities, as each defended his own position all through the period between the demise of the hotel and the birth of the village, is almost audible. Mr. Atha seems invariably to come off second best in these encounters; but in all fairness it must be said that we are usually hearing only side of the story—namely, that of Professor Poor, who left several boxes of yellowing papers stored in the upper recesses of his house. Mr. Atha, on the other hand, left neither house nor papers. In view of the leading roles these gentlemen played in the Island Realty Company, the Casino and the Manhanset Country Club, a biographical digression is in order.

Professor Poor—as he was invariably addressed—was a man of diverse talents and extraordinary energy. In many ways he resembled his colleague at Harvard, Professor Horsford of Sylvester Manor. Both were scholars, gentlemen and activists, dedicating themselves with intensity to academic and public affairs. Both were scientists—the one a chemist, the other a mathematician.

Poor was twenty when he became an instructor in mathematics at the College of the City of New York, soon transferring to The Johns Hopkins University, where he was associate professor of astronomy. He apparently spent his summers on Shelter Island, and was occupying a third-floor bedroom in the first Manhanset House when it caught fire in 1896. At the turn of the century he came back to New York City as professor of astronomy at Columbia University, where he remained for the rest of a career that was by no means merely academic. As will be abundantly evident, he never shrank from public challenges, whether to Einstein's theory of relativity, Franklin Delano Roosevelt's New Deal or the perennial proposal to build bridges to Shelter Island.

As a yachtsman he registered his 54-foot sloop *Mira* not only with the New York Yacht Club but with the equally exclusive Larchmont Yacht Club as well, along with August Belmont's 166-foot *Mineóla*, J. P. Morgan's 132-foot sloop *Columbia*, Cornelius Vanderbilt's 106-foot *Rainbow*, Sir Thomas Lipton's 135-foot *Shamrock* and His Imperial Majesty Kaiser Wilhelm's 160-foot schooner *Meteor*.[18] Skipper Poor invented the "line of position computer" which played an important role in World War I, and during that conflict he loaned his private yacht to the U. S. Navy. Author of many articles and a prolific correspondent, he also published a highly technical volume, *Men Against the Rule: A Century of Progress in Yacht Design*, an autographed copy of which may be found in the Shelter Island Library. In 1892 he married Anna Louise Easton; they had three sons, Charles Lane, Jr., Alfred Easton and Edmund Ward.

About Benjamin Atha much less information is readily available. He served as president of the Essex National Bank of Newark, New Jersey; that his principal occupation was a family metal business may be deduced circumstantially from two scraps of paper—one a bill of lading dated 1915 from the Atha Tool Company of Newark, a manufacturer of hammers, hatchets, sledges, wedges, wrenches, crowbars and rail tongs, the other a letterhead, used by his son Louis Atha, for the Titan Casting Corporation of Newark.

In any event, Benjamin Atha became the first president of the Island Realty Company and apparently had the heaviest financial stake in it, protected by a lien on the Red Cottage. His father, Henry Atha, had brought the family to the Manhanset House in the 1880s and was gratefully remembered by scores of children whom he invited to sail aboard his yacht *Wyvern*. He seems to have bought one or more lots as early as 1883, and a house in 1890. The son followed close in his father's wake, reserving all his leisure time—aside from frequent trips to Europe— for Shelter Island and, later on, its golf course.

A Tale of Two Houses

Two of Manhanset's cottages, standing almost back to back, were for many years associated with the Atha name. One was the gingerbread house on the north side of Setauket, now Gardiner Way, dating to 1873.[12] One may speculate, in the light of the tension that was to develop, that the elder Athas occupied this house until the Poors erected a three-story mansion which effectively blocked their view of Dering Harbor. In any event, Henry and Sarah Atha then moved to a cottage on Patchogue Avenue, the next street facing the hotel park, leaving the older cottage with its view of the Poor mansion to their son and his growing family.

Several years later—in 1907, to be exact—Benjamin tore down the Patchogue Avenue house to build "one of the show places in Dering Harbor"— or so it was described after a fire had destroyed it some twenty years later. Evidently this spacious new cottage, with its unrestricted view, was meant to rival in splendor the one Poor had built in 1898.

Then, in 1911, the Poor's mansion went up in flames one Sunday morning in November, about a year after the disastrous hotel fire. Live cinders from the kitchen chimney falling among the leaves that had accumulated on the roof ignited the blaze, and it was only with the assistance of Italian workers from the Casino site that any of the fine furniture could be rescued. When the fire was out, only a small auxiliary building, a garage and/or bungalow, remained intact. Several consequences followed from the event. One was the professor's fixed resolve never to roof another house with wooden shingles. Another was an agreement not to obstruct Atha's view of the water by constructing another house on that site.

It is barely possible that the latter agreement has become somehow confused with a stipulation regarding the Athas' other house, but in fact Poor never rebuilt on the old site. Perhaps he already had his eye on the location commanding both Dering Harbor and Greenport Channel, which was to become known as Poor's Point.

The other stipulation laid down by Atha, which Poor keenly resented, appears in their compact to salvage the old hotel property and transfer it to the Island Realty Company. Hear Professor Poor's version:

> Before making this transfer Mr. Poor and Mr. Atha had many talks regarding the layout and improvement of the property. Mr. Atha stated that his reason for joining in the purchase was to keep the view from his cottage on Patchogue open.... The condition inserted by Mr. Atha for his personal benefit rendered practically valueless for selling purposes one and one-half acres of the most valuable land of the Company [whereas] the condition inserted by Mr. Poor [namely to tear up what is now Shore Road, about which more will be heard] would have benefitted twelve cottage owners as well as Mr. Poor, and would have cost the Company practically

nothing.... When in 1914 Mr. Poor purchased his cottage site [that is, the three acres of Poor's Point], Mr. Atha insisted on inserting in the deed a restrictive clause covering this [and] greatly reducing the value of the land.

Ultimately, as we shall see, the house of Poor triumphed over the house of Atha. When the latter's house burned down in 1926—several years after the family had left Dering Harbor—Professor Poor bought the empty lot and divided it between the two adjacent cottages, which were soon to be remodeled and renamed Eastgate and Westgate. Of course, Mr. Atha might have called the triumph as empty as the lot, since the two open views which he championed remain unrestricted to this day.

The first decade of the twentieth century, which had begun so auspiciously for Manhanset Manor and the Manhanset House, ended in ashes. But the end of the nineteenth century had not been, as some people feared, the end of the world. Most of the stockholders in Island Realty had a keen personal interest as well as a financial stake in the future of Shelter Island. They included men like Carl Pickhardt, of the German town group, and Artemas Ward, whose summer home dominated the channel near the South Ferry. Even the New York architect, George Freeman, who was charged with designing the projected Casino, became a stockholder. As for the undeveloped real estate, a revised survey based on subdivision into one-acre lots was ordered; and it was specified, no doubt at Poor's insistence, that any new building was to be characterized by "a certain architecture and beauty."

As a matter of fact, the "ball of fire" that descended on the hotel in 1910 marked the real transition from one century to another. The end of the hotel became the beginning of the Village. One man's vision of Locust Point, as a resort with a summer hotel at its center, had given way forty years later to another man's vision, of a community of summer cottages. Whereas the former vision fed on publicity, the latter vision would be nurtured by privacy. But the weaning process would not be easy.

Chapter VI

THE MINI-MUNICIPALITY
1910-20

GROUND WAS BROKEN for the new Casino in 1911. In the idiom of
the day, "it promises to be classy." The site chosen ran along the bluff above
the Greenport channel, just to the east of the former hotel.[1] The proposed
clubhouse—by contrast to its elegant predecessor—was to be as nonflammable
and as functional as possible. This meant, in the first place, no frame
construction. The specifications included solid brick, stucco-covered walls
topped with a red tile roof. In the second place, there were to be no overnight
accommodations! Obviously Professor Poor was peering over the architect's
shoulder.

The design was "contemporary." At the basement level there were to be
an *al fresco* cafe, locker rooms for men and women, a chauffeurs' dining room,
kitchen and pantries. The first floor would contain deep piazzas, lounges,
breakfast and dining rooms, a bridge-whist parlor and offices. The top floor was
set aside for the superintendent's private quarters and storage space. Originally
Poor had assigned the management of the completed Casino to a John Scofield
of New Rochelle, but this appointment was vetoed by Atha.

The gala opening in 1912 did not take place until mid-August, a month
behind schedule. Although the summer season was practically over, a lengthy
description of the event, complete with large photograph was featured on the
front page of the *Suffolk Weekly Times*. From it we learn that hundreds of guests
participated in a full weekend of receptions, teas, dinners and balls; that six
yachts belonging to the New York Yacht Club raced from New London to
Greenport; and that there was another race on Sunday afternoon for a cup
donated by Mrs. Poor.

There is absolutely no ground for believing that Will Rogers enlivened
this brilliant occasion with his dry cowboy humor. On the contrary, there is
every reason to suspect that Professor Poor would have objected strenuously to
his presence. But at the time of the great humorist's death in a plane crash it
was recalled that his visit to Shelter Island in 1912 coincided with a drive to
reduce the number of deer, whose foraging in fields and gardens had roused the
populace to vengeful counter measures. Coming upon a party of hunters in his
"tin lizzie," Mr. Rogers received permission to join them. He succeeded in
having himself bowled over by a buck—whether inadvertently or otherwise is

not entirely clear—and managed to capture a live fawn, all of which made excellent publicity.[2]

The Casino was not at all interested in that kind of national advertisement. As a matter of fact, the very name "Casino" seems to have been quietly dropped in favor of "Manhanset Club," perhaps because the Monte Carlo flavor of the more exotic term (which also means "summer house") was deemed inappropriate or misleading. In its constitution, probably written by Mr. Poor, the clearly stated purpose of the unincorporated association was to provide a social center for the members and to offer facilities for healthy outdoor activities such as tennis, golf and yachting. Bowling and bridge were undoubtedly rainy-day substitutes. Two new tennis courts were indeed constructed before the following summer.

Despite a very small membership, the annual fees were kept low: residents $30, non-residents—defined as persons living more than a mile away—$15, associates $10. At this modestly exclusive level the new center "operated successfully," as President Poor later wrote, for three years. At the conclusion of the 1913 season there was even a net balance of $299, thanks no doubt to the year-end liberality of a few members. The moderately successful replacement of the hotel by a community club did not, however, begin to solve all the practical problems inherited from the defunct Manhanset Corporation. Such mundane matters as the ownership and continued operation of essential utilities—the power plant, the water mains, the roadbeds—still had to be resolved. Experienced personnel from previous seasons were probably available for re-employment—but under whose authority and direction?

The Island Realty Company had been hastily organized for the primary purpose of holding and managing real estate, as its name implies. Its secondary function was to sell land and thus liquidate the $45,000 mortgage held by the Corn Exchange Bank. Furthermore, Island Realty was scheduled to "self-destruct" upon completion of its limited mission, presumably within three years. Actually the process took seven years. Meanwhile it not only had to cope with a power plant but found itself back in the hotel business!

The solid evidence for this strange turn of events is found in the first annual report, in June 1913, to the Island Realty stockholders, which states that the "Casino Annex, or Club House... was completed and was formally opened on August 10, 1912"—apparently to coincide with the grand opening of the Casino itself. The story of this "Little Hotel," as it was dubbed, is almost as intriguing as that of the grand hotel to which it once belonged. Moreover, the building still exists!

This particular annex was originally located on the south side of Patchogue Avenue, across from the hotel's two tennis courts, between Eastgate cottage and the present Village hall. Several years before the fateful fire, it had been constructed—or possibly remodeled—as the last residential unit of the Manhanset House. Being at a good distance from the conflagration, it had escaped unscathed.[3] Now it stood bereft, as though pleading for adoption by the neighboring cottages.

The Athas, whose fine big house was only two doors away, responded to the silent appeal and undertook to rekindle this small spark of hotel business. Just why they did so remains unclear. Prolonged vacancy would, of course, have constituted both a considerable hazard to the building and a great waste; but how many uses are there for a 24-bedroom "cottage"? Besides, there seemed to be a real need for a guest house to supplement the Casino, even though Professor Poor could be counted on to oppose the idea. Whatever the reasons, responsibility for the Little Hotel, and for the utilities, was shouldered by Benjamin Atha and his son Louis.

The Three-Legged Manhanset Club

It was not long before an ingenious idea began to take shape in someone's fertile mind. Why not federate or congregate all social activities in a full-fledged country club? No doubt the reactivation of the golf course was the center of the concept. The term "federate" accurately describes this proposed non-merger, whereby the Casino would remain a private club while providing the aegis for both a public guest house and the golf course, which was about to lose its original clubhouse. The scheme quite obviously endeavored to reconcile the divergent interests of both Poor and Atha, while appealing to everybody else on the sensible ground of greater economy of operation.

It is quite likely that Professor Poor resisted this arrangement as long as he could. His plans for the Casino definitely excluded overnight guests. He envisaged it as a local social center, not a public facility, in a residential community that was already well equipped with bedrooms. However, he found himself up against some hard facts, such as the physical presence of a substantial building containing twenty-four bedrooms, the need for a broader base to support a golf course—and above all, the way the Athas were using the Island Realty Company to run "their" Little Hotel.

It is not clear whether the other cottage owners ever fully shared either Poor's personal convictions or his willingness to dig into his own pocket to subsidize the Casino. Probably they tried to avoid taking sides. In any event, not only was the Manhanset Country Club incorporated in June 1914, but Benjamin Atha skillfully took advantage of Professor Poor's prolonged trip to Europe that summer to lift the Little Hotel bodily, move it several hundred feet and actually link it to the Casino by means of an arcade![4]

Upon his return to the States, Poor was understandably enraged; but the deed, which for him overshadowed the outbreak of World War I, was a *fait accompli*. The transition had been effected by a Newark firm for the sum of $750. Two plumbers were employed for eleven days, at $4 a day, to lay new water mains. The new annex was enlarged to accommodate thirty-four guest bedrooms, "electrified," stuccoed to match the Casino and furnished with a red tile roof, no doubt to mollify the professor. The electrification is noteworthy because it coincided with the wiring of the first of the private cottages, and one of the original ones,[5] by the same contractor.

By the end of the year a plan of operation for the new club had been finally worked out by a special committee of Casino members, namely, Adolf Kuttroff, Louis M. Atha and Charles L. Morse. In an ensuing prospectus it was conceded that the original proposal for a simple club with golf course had been "modified" by an "addition," which was "made necessary by the demand for rooms for Club guests, and to meet the requirements of the Liquor Tax law."

But Poor's battle was not entirely lost. The next significant step was the incorporation of a separate service agency, the Manhanset Hotel Company, which would lease certain facilities from both Island Realty and the Casino, but *not* hold title to any real estate. Its role would be limited to the management of the guest house and the operation of the club's kitchen, bar and dining room. It would also be responsible for the utility services to the entire community. In the blunt words of Poor's subsequent "general statement," "This hotel company was to be an Atha concern, with some [Artemas] Ward money; the feeling being that Atha being entirely responsible for the difficulties, he should assume the entire risk." A parallel effort to take Island Realty completely out of Atha hands soon became evident.

The formula was logical enough in theory but proved excessively complicated in practice. The hotel's guests, for instance, were permitted to eat in a restricted area of the dining room. The remainder of the club, however, was off limits to non-members without guest privileges. Keeping the accounts straight was to prove even more troublesome than monitoring the people.

The final element in the tripartite package—also a Benjamin Atha project—was the extension of the golf course to the front door of the Casino. This was accomplished by cutting two more fairways through the woods so that players could begin and end their rounds just across the road from the club's tennis courts and locker rooms. This eliminated the fairly long trek by car to the former clubhouse—Thomas Dering's Colonial farmhouse—which resumed its function as the private dwelling of Dr. Frederick Prime.

Amid this welter of rearrangements, Island Realty succeeded in consummating two major land transactions, for which Professor Poor took the credit. Early in 1913 a "wealthy millowner" from Passaic, New Jersey, Samuel Hird, bought one and a quarter acres of unimproved land adjacent to Julia Havens' Creek and began building a very handsome summer home on the Dering Harbor shore for his wife and their ten children.[6] Before he was twenty years old he had left England with his fiancée and her mother, to enact the classic American success story of bold initiative, hard work, good sense and good fortune. After a stint in the weaving mills of Germantown— Pennsylvania, not Manhanset Manor!—he took charge of a plant in New Jersey which specialized in producing blue serge cloth, which happened just then to be the most popular fabric for women's skirts. The forerunner of blue denim! The family first summered on Fisher's Island but found it too remote. According to his son, Henry E. Hird, the two oldest daughters were deputized by their father to look for a more convenient place. Their recommendation was Shelter Island.

The following year an artist from New York City and Sandy Spring, Maryland, named Milton Bancroft, bought both a guest cottage[7] and the abandoned chapel, the latter for $650 to be used as a studio. Not much is known about his professional career except that he was a member of the Pennsylvania Academy of Fine Arts at Philadelphia and that he was commissioned to paint some murals for the 1914 Pan American Exposition at San Francisco. When the United States entered World War I, he volunteered to serve with the YMCA and was charged with decorating the Y's "huts" in France. It is presumably he who replaced the rose window in the chapel's front wall with a much larger "gothic" window for the sake of the northern light, and who disposed of the ecclesiastical furniture.

Despite the war in Europe, the Manhanset Country Club got off to a promising start in the summer of 1915, with the usual fanfare and a blizzard of brochures. The summer community could congratulate itself on having taken its future into its own hands, thus foreclosing the danger of unpleasant commercialization. The new club owned its premises, albeit mortgaged, and had a ten-year lease on the new eighteen-hole golf course. The hotel company was functioning under local auspices and the Island Realty Company was the legal successor to Shelter Island Park's remaining acreage. The big wharf was repaired and the bathing beach was enhanced by the addition of a diving float, a shoot-the-chute, showers and lockers. The future of the Dering Harbor community seemed assured.

Harmony, however, was short-lived. A well-meaning disposition to keep costs at a minimum had been the reason for federating the diverse activities. But in so small a group of interested participants it became impossible to prevent the affairs of the various agencies, including their financial accounts, from becoming hopelessly entangled. All three were involved in claims and counterclaims, especially against the hotel company and its management. The real trouble was that the little Manhanset "army" had too many four-star generals functioning without a high command. According to the presence or absence of responsible officers in the interlocking directorates, successive orders tended to conflict and bills for the hotel, for instance, were not infrequently referred to the Casino account, or vice versa.

The tug of war between those who favored a public hotel and those who preferred a private club was still being carried on. Economic considerations argued in favor of a small but profitable hotel enterprise; social preferences—at any rate Professor Poor's—urged maximum privacy, even at the risk of having personally to cover consequent deficits. It was not simply a question of hotel vs. club, but of conflicting personalities. Mr. Atha and his son Louis dominated the hotel company, and Mr. Poor served on its board. The actual president of the country club was Artemas Ward—who, as president of King Motors from 1913 to 1920, was involved in the burgeoning auto industry—but Professor Poor was vice president of the club and Mr. Atha was a trustee! The possibility of friction was never absent. Professor Poor, as was his wont in such circumstances, applied himself to finding a logical formula for clarifying the relationships between the realty company, the hotel company and the country club. The nub of it was that Island Realty—Benjamin Atha, president—would remain aloof from all "operations" except the rental and maintenance of the two remaining guest cottages, the Red and the Yellow; the hotel company—Louis Atha, manager—would pay a flat fee of $350 per year to the realty company for its lease of the utilities and an annual rental of $750 to the country club for the use of the annex.

Establishing the Village

But the fertile mind of Professor Poor was still restless. He soon set forth a much more radical solution, which no doubt he had been contemplating for some time. That the hotel company proposed to charge him $75 per month for electricity—during evening hours only!—so outraged him that he continued using oil lamps in his brand-new house.[8] Why not, he proposed, establish a village government to take responsibility for all public services?

It would be interesting to know exactly when the idea first struck him. At his instigation the postal designation had already been changed from Manhanset Manor to Dering Harbor, largely to avoid further confusion with Manhasset, Long Island. There had been no strong opposition to this move—which, in fact, met with an amiable echo across the channel. "The name Dering Harbor is full of sentiment and greatly admired," declared the *Suffolk Weekly*

Times.[2] This sentiment probably reflected the feelings of Professor Poor, who had served as official postmaster since the fire and would later assume the title of deputy sheriff when weekend motor traffic became a problem.

There was nothing in the aforementioned article to indicate whether the admiration was for the harbor itself or for the man for whom it is named. Thomas Dering had come to Sylvester Manor in 1760, after his marriage to Mary Sylvester, and had thoroughly identified himself with Shelter Island, serving for a time as town supervisor. He was a close friend of the famous British evangelist George Whitefield, acting as his host during a visit to the Island in 1764.

Whatever the reasons for adopting the name, the cottage owners unanimously agreed to apply for incorporation under a recently revised state law, which Poor had carefully researched. "The advantages are many," he assured his fellow residents, proceeding to list them under three general headings: first, local control over utilities and roads; second, direct control over property assessments and taxes as opposed to Town control; and third, "the solution of many of the difficulties at Dering Harbor"—no doubt a reference to the Atha management of the Island Realty and the Manhanset Hotel companies.

A formal vote on the matter was to be conducted by the supervisor and the clerk of the Town of Shelter Island on September 7, 1916, after which a temporary Village clerk would be appointed for the proper election of Village officers.

Then a disheartening obstacle appeared with the realization that at least ten ballots were required by law—and that so many male votes could not be mustered. Then, as now, real estate titles were often held in the wife's name, but all this was happening before the advent of women's suffrage. One sole exception was discovered in the law—namely, that women property owners were eligible to vote in matters of municipal incorporation. It was therefore, thanks to the votes of three women that the measure passed, although those same women could not participate in the subsequent election of the village officials !

At the first election, held two months later, there were four offices to be filled, and exactly four registered voters were present. Mr. Tarrant Putnam became president, a title which state law later changed to mayor. Professor Poor became treasurer and collector of taxes. Messrs. Adolf Schwarzmann and W. Paul Pickhardt, both of Little Germany, were the two other trustees. For many years thereafter, the annual election of the smallest incorporated village in the Empire State brought in no more than from six to ten eligible voters.

The choice of Tarrant Putnam as president proved to be a good one, all the more since he was very reluctant to accept the office. Well along in years, he was planning to transfer his summer residence from Shelter Island to Islip, Long Island, if in fact he had not already done so. The reason for this decision is unknown, but the commuting distance from New York City, the burning of the Manhanset House and the consequent closing of the New York Yacht Club Station may have influenced him. However, he still owned the cottage he had purchased from Frank Robinson in 1896 for $4,500. So he permitted himself to be drafted.

Putnam, a prominent lawyer with offices on lower Broadway in New York City, had no irons in the Manhanset fire, or ashes, and was deeply respected by all who knew him. In short, he was a perfect buffer between Charles Lane Poor and Benjamin Atha. The well-kept files of his official correspondence reveal that he also knew how to attend to the business of the Village promptly, calmly and judiciously. Neither prejudice nor ambition is discernible in his dealings.

In addition to his cottage, Putnam owned a very small lot—only two-tenths of an acre—which was part of his estate at his death in 1926 and was eventually bought by the golf club. He also owned a farm in East Marion on the North Fork and since 1885 had been a member of the swank Larchmont Yacht Club, where both his mainsail yacht *Dione* and a thirty-foot launch were listed. During his term, and for many years thereafter, most of the Village paper work was transacted in Manhattan.

The first business meeting, however, was held in the country club on November 7. The first business of the tiny municipality was the appointment of a village clerk at $5 per month, an attorney and a health officer—namely, the Island's physician, Dr. Benjamin. Four departmental budgets were established under the general headings of roads, health, light and water, as well as a catchall fund (consistently misspelled "contigent"). Authorization was granted to negotiate with the Island Realty Company for acquisition of water, gas, electric light and power plants, piers and sewers, parks and roadbeds at a top cost of $5,000. As Island Realty had already set that same price on this same package, and Professor Poor was treasurer of both parties, the deal was soon concluded. Of course, capital funds had to be raised, not only to pay for the purchase but to cover the repair, maintenance and operation of these facilities. This was accomplished by seeking voters' consent to issuing a series of bonds ranging from $500 for highways to $8,500 for lighting. The result was six in favor of the bond issues, none opposed.

In his brief address at the dedication of the new Village hall in 1931, Mayor Poor summed up the condition of the Village and consequent actions in those early days:

> The roads were in poor condition, the water supply was inadequate, the tanks and pumps old and liable to fail at any moment, and the only lighting system available to cottagers was an antiquated acetylene gas plant. Before the opening of the next season the Trustees had purchased and revamped the electric light plant, originally built to supply the main floor of the

Manhanset Hotel, and had organized the first public electric light service on Shelter Island. On account of drastic requirements of the Public Service Commission, however, the plant could only be operated for a single shift of not more than eight hours a day, so that light was available only during the evening hours. The wells, pumping plant and mains of the old hotel company were purchased; the wells protected, and the whole system made safe. All of these immediate essentials were costly, and the bonded and floating indebtedness of the Village soon reached an amount of some $25,000.

Other major actions in the first years were the adoption X>f an official Village map, the first really new survey since 1872, and the purchase for $2,000 of a rather decrepit building to serve, after renovation, as an engineer's residence, Village hall and post office.[10] ° The most persistent and vexing agenda items from the beginning and for a long time to come were the numerous complaints regarding water and light bills, meters, rates and utility services in general, not to mention the touchy question of delinquent cottage accounts. Distribution of acetylene gas was discontinued early in 1918. As people became more accustomed to using electric lights, they asked for current earlier in the day and later in the evening, but grumbled about the rates.

Second Poor House, First Towl House

Meanwhile, despite a brief bout with hard times, new cottages were being built and several more families were moving in.[11] Two years had elapsed between Professor Poor's purchase of his new lot on Locust Point and the receipt of a clear title. Not satisfied with a quitclaim from Island Realty and "acting on the advice of the Lawyers' Title Insurance Company," he had bought quitclaims "from all parties who might have an interest in old rights of way." There must be at least a dozen such deeds on file in Riverhead! At last the Poors were able to move into their "magnificent new residence," which had been completed in less than six months. Its impressive breadth dominated the point of land where the waters of Dering Harbor met those of Greenport Channel, a piece of the shore that the hotel had always refused to sell. Some were fond of saying that the fashionably low, and sprawling white structure had been built around a handsome front door taken from a house dating to 1831, which had been demolished in Greenport. This fine cottage, finished in 1915, was crowned with a slate roof and called Eastward, not for the direction it faced but for the combined middle names—Easton and Ward—of the two younger sons, just as Laneholm had been named for eldest. [12]

There were newcomers to the community at this time, some from the

Heights, where they had been renting cottages for several seasons. Among them were the three Towl brothers, who in little more than a decade erected three fine summer homes set on large lawns among many trees. From now on the trustees, with Charles Lane Poor in the forefront, would see to it that the original concept of hundreds of little bungalows on lots 60 feet wide by 100 feet deep would never be realized.

Forrest Towl, the first to arrive, was a graduate engineer, a pipeline specialist and Standard Oil executive who had developed a technique for raising the temperature of oil so that it would flow through conduits up to twenty times more rapidly than cold oil. He chose a site next to Samuel Hird and in 1916 began to build a spacious cottage.[13] In the following year he was given the task of laying a one-inch pipeline across Scotland to carry a wartime supply of oil to the British navy, for which feat he received a special commendation from London. With Manhanset's chapel now a studio, he continued to be a very active member of the Union Chapel committee in the Heights.

The second Towl, Allan, first rented a cottage on Patchogue Avenue and subsequently bought the Tarrant Putnam house next door to it. A dozen years later, after buying the adjacent lot along Shore Road—where Poor's first house had stood—he demolished the old cottage to build a large new one very much like his brother's.[14] Also like his brother, he had a long and notable career in oil transportation, first as an executive in the Oklahoma Pipeline Company, later in Pennsylvania. He became a president of the Dering Harbor Golf Club and, as a member of the Yacht Club, sailed the first *Star* class boat in local waters. The third brother, Burr Towl, associated with the New York Transit Company, also rented at first, then bought the Red Cottage before building a new house on Locust Point Avenue.[15] The two new Towl houses were not built until 1928.

While the Village was learning to fend for itself, the overextended Manhanset Country Club was close to drowning in debt. The golf course was paying its own way but all else operated in the red, despite such last-gasp measures as the opening of a gift shop in the clubhouse to attract the general public ! The handful of really affluent members—with the loyal exception of Professor Poor—became increasingly reluctant to subsidize an operation for the benefit of transient guests who seemed to claim a disproportionate share of the staff's time. Other members blamed the new management for opening the club too early in the season at the behest of a few, or for letting it become a kind of glorified real estate office. Even Professor Poor observed that the menus were needlessly elaborate—four-course luncheons when three courses would do! In short, the attempt to satisfy everybody was doomed to failure.

It would be easy to suggest that World War I was to blame for Manhanset's financial predicament, but to do so would not be accurate. The summer of 1917 turned out to be Shelter Island's "biggest season on record." Hyperbole? Or was it the gratifying result of a well-mounted publicity campaign by the local Chamber of Commerce? Guests were reported to be sleeping in hallways and billiard rooms at the Prospect House, and even in automobiles. Hundreds were turned away. People were coming from the midwest and California. Fuel rationing had little or no effect on this influx. Heating fuel posed no problem for summer resorts, and the long lines of automobiles waiting their turn at the ferry seemed in no dire need of gasoline. The following winter, be it noted, the channel between Greenport and the Island was frozen solid for forty-six days; the Manhanset wharf was shattered. For the first time in history autos could be driven across the ice.

Nearby marine industries were booming. When Thomas A. Edison spent several weeks at the Greenport House in September 1917 on U. S. Navy business, the townspeople had the added pleasure of seeing two old friends who came to visit him—Henry Ford and John Burroughs. The great naturalist "with his clean, white flowing beard made a most unusual and charming appearance, as he sat on the hotel porch in one of the easy chairs."[16] It was in the same month that first-class postage went from two to three cents.

The Club Collapses

Meanwhile some fairly strenuous efforts were being made to salvage the country club, for instance by trying to merge several small clubs, including the Heights golf course, into a still larger one. The request of the U. S. Navy for the use of the club house as a service center was turned down rather than suffer an invasion by all ranks—though naval officers would be welcomed as guest members! Nothing came of that invitation. Finally, in November 1917 a petition of voluntary dissolution was filed by the trustees, a receiver was appointed and in due course a public sale was announced. All the assets, with an estimated value of $40,000 but burdened with an equal amount of indebtedness, were divided into six parcels and auctioned off the following August in front of the First National Bank in Greenport. The club had not lasted nearly as long as the hotel.

Professor Poor, still determined to fend off undesirable strangers, bought up the Casino with furniture and fixtures, servants' housing and a horse for a little more than $6,000. The Annex, which had been heavily mortgaged by Mr. Atha to a Mrs. Lucy Drexel Dahlgren of Philadelphia, was offered separately and eventually bought up by Artemas Ward. Since no one seemed to want the golf course, William T. Barr, a newcomer to Dering Harbor but a golf enthusiast and expert, offered $3 for the lease and $175 for the equipment in order to keep the course open. He subsequently renewed the lease, rented the Casino as a clubhouse and renamed it the Dering Harbor Golf Club. Thereafter the name Manhanset disappeared from the Village except as the designation of one of its main avenues.

To hold the Casino property Professor Poor and his partners immediately formed another agency, the Triton Investing Corporation, of which he was treasurer. No record of Triton's legal incorporation can be found in Albany. Apparently there were only two other partners, W. P. Pickhardt and Artemas Ward, both of whom later resigned, at least as directors.[17] The partnership dissolved with the sale of the Casino several years later, after the erection of the present golf clubhouse near the center of the links.

Still another holding agency, this one legally registered, came into existence about the same time as Triton. Called Unity Investing Corporation, it was set up by a Wall Street law firm acting for Professor Poor. The official certificate issued to three lawyers gives blanket authorization to engage in real estate dealings on a nominal investment of $500. But a letter from Professor Poor to the firm[18] contains clear directives, first concerning the purchase of a Poor mortgage; second, for the sale of certain Island Realty assets to Samuel Hird, Forrest Towl, John Mason Knox[19] and the Unity company itself; and third, for the foreclosure of Island Realty and auction of its remaining land in reasonably large plots as soon as possible.

The liquidation of Island Realty had been under consideration for some time. As successor to the Manhanset Improvement Corporation, it had been no more profitable to its shareholders than the country club. The same individuals were usually involved, except that the Athas seem to have been left out of Unity. (Could that have been the reason for the name?) The main purpose of the new entity was no doubt mainly legal, but a clash of interests and of personalities was plainly apparent. Both Poor and Pickhardt had dissociated themselves from Island Realty. And it was at about this time that Benjamin Atha sold his own two houses, abandoning the field to Professor Poor.

During this period of realignment the cottages and unimproved acreage belonging to Island Realty were divided on a pro rata basis among the big shareholders or sold off in sizable blocks to Samuel Hird and Forrest Towl.[20] Kurd's lawyer, Stephen Sturges, delayed matters for a while by refusing to accept a survey based on the old Bateman map which showed many unopened streets. Professor Poor, who rightly claimed full credit for clinching the deal with Mr. Hird, contended quite correctly that the title was not really clouded by the old survey. He entered into a heated exchange with the adamant attorney, who finally wrote in obvious exasperation, "If you do not know the law well enough to understand what I have written, you could consult your lawyers and direct them to reply to my letters. Mr. Hird will not accept an unmarketable title, and if you wish to sell the land to him it will be necessary for some responsible party to contract to deliver a marketable title to the land. Why waste time?"

The words "responsible party" refer to the fact that Professor Poor at that time was neither an official nor a director of Island Realty Company. Somehow the problem was resolved. The Company finally expired in 1920, and Unity Investing Corporation emerged holding only a part of the golf course and the area later known as Land's End—in short, the eastern section of the Village. For a few intervening years Unity, with William Ban-as president, functioned as the legal successor to the golf club. When the new clubhouse was erected in 1926, legal title to the acreage which lay within the village boundaries passed from the Unity Investing Corporation to the Dering Harbor Golf Club, Inc.

The sale of Locust Point's two hundred acres into private hands, as projected by the original purchasers, was now virtually complete but by no means in the manner they had foreseen. The trail was littered with the relics many incorporations and reorganizations: Shelter Island Park Association, Manhanset Improvement Corporation, Island Realty Company, Manhanset Hotel Company and Manhanset Country Club and, finally, the Triton and Unity Investing corporations. Much money and time had been invested at various stages; much money and time had been lost, but not entirely in vain. The biggest loss seems to have been the magnetic glamour of the big hotel. In 1919, when Mary Pickford and Douglas Fairbanks motored to the North Fork in a "superb limousine," they dined at Steve's Restaurant in Greenport—but did not deign to visit Shelter Island. The Village of Dering Harbor was in the process of becoming pretty much what its new mayor desired: a quiet, intimate community of well-to-do cottagers—and their invited guests.

Chapter VII

MAYOR POOR TAKES THE HELM—
HARD ALEE
1920-30

THE VASTLY ALTERED status of Dering Harbor is well illustrated by a letter that arrived in June 1921 from Rochester, New York, addressed simply to The Exclusive Cottage Colony, Shelter Island, New York. It requested "descriptive matter pertaining to cottages for rent, stating prices and conveniences included." What the tiny village had sacrificed in one kind of prestige it seems to have gained in another.

The task of erasing the scars left by the incineration of the grand hotel was almost finished. By the time Poor succeeded Putnam as mayor in 1919, a board of trustees was firmly in control of all financial affairs and public services in what was literally a one-horse town. Five more years would elapse before a motor truck replaced Dering Harbor's faithful horse and wagon !

Island Realty, as already noted, had been liquidated in 1920 after four cottagers bought up all the remaining acreage adjacent to their other holdings. According to the new mayor, "The disappearance of dominant corporate ownership was accompanied by a complete change in sentiment among property owners. A spirit of cooperation and interest in village affairs at once developed... The remaining outbuildings of the old Manhanset House, which Island Realty had hung onto, were torn down and the land improved. Old stables, colored servants' quarters and other buildings (ice house, etc.) which had cost tens of thousands of dollars, were scrapped and sold for lumber or firewood."[1]

No new cottages were built at this time but many of the existing ones were extensively refurbished. By the end of 1921 all houses were equipped with electricity, far ahead of the Heights and the rest of the Island. The limitations of this service did not escape criticism, however. Two major sources of complaint were the continued reliance on an antiquated, steam-driven dynamo, installed originally to light only the main floor of the hotel, and the strict observance of the Public Service Commission's regulations specifying an eight-hour day for employees. Since the small community was not ready to invest in a new power plant or to engage additional personnel, there was electric power only in the evening hours.

The decrepit sewage system posed a more urgent problem. The great ice storm of 1918 had shattered the hotel wharf and smashed the sewer pipe that ran under it into Greenport channel. The wharf itself was now out of service and expendable, but sewage disposal was a necessity. A year earlier the second sewer line, which ran westward into Dering Harbor, had become clogged, causing Mr. Knox to complain of the stench between his house and his neighbor's.[2] A Village meeting was called in September 1920 and in remarkably short order the property owners had agreed unanimously to discontinue the old lines and to install "individual Waring systems," or cesspools.

At the same meeting they agreed in principle to the construction of a "recreation pier" at the foot of Aquebogue, now Yoco, Avenue. This seems to have been a pet project of the new mayor, who had previously offered to sell his dock, the former Manhanset bathing dock, for the purpose. When the matter was submitted for final approval two years later, the pier was rejected six to five.

Official actions were now being taken in a rather haphazard order, as dictated by necessity or convenience, but they were taken. Board meetings were convened with regular irregularity several times a year, either in the old "Hall" or in someone's mid-Manhattan office. At no time from then until now do the recorded minutes ever offer much more than the bare factual bones of problems presented and decisions taken. No paper was wasted in recording the substance of the discussions or providing a modicum of background information. But the records leave no doubt that the trustees generally preferred to reduce their inherited responsibilities to an absolute minimum rather than assume new ones. On the whole, a healthy sign!

End of the Bedtime Blinks, Fortunately No Electric Toothbrushes

The provision of light and water was a constant source of irritation and contention. Thick account books, far more voluminous than the official minutes, constitute a substantial part of the Village archives during this period. The obligatory installation of meters eliminated some arguments over the quantity of water actually consumed—but gave rise to others, especially in cases where it was unclear whether the utilities were to paid by the owner or his tenant, or divided between them.

In response to reiterated pleas, it was announced that electric current would be turned on at 6:30 P.M., "except on dark and stormy days, when they [the lights] are to be turned on as much earlier as necessary. Except on Fridays and Saturdays the lights are to be shut off at 10:40 P.M., the blink to be given at 10:30." On weekends the warning blink came at midnight, and it was lights out ten minutes later.

A couple of years later arrangements were at last concluded with the Shelter Island Light and Power Company, first organized in 1922, to supplement the Village output, thus permitting 24-hour service, whereupon "the bedtime blinks passed into oblivion."[3] Earlier efforts to merge the two services had failed, possibly because Dering Harbor prided itself on having brought the first public electric generator to the Island. Water-metering continued, along with the monthly billings, until the early 1970s; thereafter "free water" was provided by simply tucking the costs into the overall budget.

The roads required considerable attention. By 1919 the narrow street along Dering Harbor shore was made a one-way thoroughfare. Before that, Professor Poor not only advocated closing it entirely but had taken the ill-advised personal initiative of plowing up a stretch. He always contended that the sole condition of his support of the purchase of the old hotel property by Island Realty was a stipulation to discontinue the road along the shore, whereas Benjamin Atha's stipulation applied solely to the view from his own front porch. He was aggrieved that Atha's selfish stipulation had been honored, whereas his own unselfish one had not. Poor may have intended to replace the road with a scenic footpath, similar to the attractive promenade on the Heights side of the harbor, which today remains a totally disused right of way across private lawns. However, a court order instituted by other cottage owners, Mr. Putnam included, forced him to restore the paving as it had been.

Many proposed roads existed only on maps as the stillborn ghost of projects now defunct. Other streets were being reclaimed by the woodland through which they had been cut. Greenport Avenue, for example, was originally conceived to serve as a main artery sweeping through the center of a populous Shelter Island Park but never became much more than a wagon track from the hotel to the distant barn and dump, now buried deep in the woods. It was allowed to disappear. Some other "thoroughfares" became dead ends—for example, South Street, which today stops abruptly at the two former carriage houses bordering close on Julia Havens' Creek. Even the streets already lined with cottages were narrowed from a theoretical breadth of sixty feet to twelve by the simple expedient of allotting additional land to the abutting owners for a modest fee. The main advantage of this decision was to transfer the onus of roadside maintenance from public to private initiative. A close look at many of the old deeds clearly reveals these inexpensive enlargements. In one instance, the price for the footage—measuring 60 by 24 feet—was exactly $50.

Similar treatment was accorded the alleys, or service roads, which were designed to run parallel to the streets and behind the cottages. The very first Village ordinance—ten years after incorporation!—declared the alley between Patchogue and Setauket "forever closed to public use" in order to build the elegant new Village hall athwart its eastern end. Allan Towl's house on Shore Road already sealed off the same alley's western end. Without further official action, all cottage owners were invited to take the initiative in moving their property lines to the center of any alleyway, existent or nonexistent. Deeds to the division of the nonexistent alley north of old Patchogue were not formally recorded until 1975.

Meanwhile, in 1922 practically all the streets were renamed, for no discernible reason—although a proposal to that effect had been made shortly after the Village was founded. Only Locust Point Road retained its identity. West Sylvester Road along the harbor became Shore Road right up to the Village hall, thus swallowing Patchogue Avenue as well. Gardiner Avenue, which probably originated as a wagon track from Sylvester Manor to Locust Point and was later improved to serve as the Town's route to the hotel wharf, became Manhanset Avenue. Setauket became Gardiner Way. Mattituck became Yoco—a name that hardly does justice to an exclusive community, much less a great Indian chief.[4]

Religion Out, Greek Revival In

In some respects the biggest change of all was the removal of the Manhanset Chapel in 1924. Back in 1890, it had been erected with a charter all its own. After the hotel fire, Milton Bancroft had bought it for an art studio. Now it was to enter upon an eight-week overland odyssey to a new site and still another career, this time at the corner of State Road and Duvall Street, not far from the Presbyterian church. It had been bought from Bancroft by the local chapter of the Junior Order of United American Mechanics, a men's benevolent association that had played an increasingly prominent role since coming to the Island in 1896. One of its stated aims was "to maintain and promote the interests of Americans and to shield them from the depressing effects of foreign competition"; another was to support the public school system of the USA and "to prevent sectarian interference therewith and uphold the reading of the Holy Bible therein."[5] For years the fraternal order had occupied meetings rooms on the second floor of an old building diagonally opposite the new site. These they now leased to the Town as they carefully laid foundations for the chapel.

Just before spring arrived, the big move from the hilltop where the church had stood for thirty-four years was begun. Progress was extremely slow, over roads churned into mud. Large branches had to be lopped off the trees along Manhanset Avenue. Nearly two weeks were consumed in pushing through the woods to the southern edge of the Village. As the ungainly structure then crept over "Mrs. Farlow's broad acres toward Benjamin's corner, [it was] plainly visible from the beach road a half-mile away."[6] Dr. Benjamin, the universally respected town physician whose early interest in bicycles and automobiles has been noted, lived near the intersection where Manhanset Avenue meets Manwaring Road. Here the chapel turned briefly west, then lumbered directly across lots to the new site, where it received a fresh coat of paint—tan with dark brown trim. The only damage it suffered was a "slight racking," which jarred loose the small rear room.

Landmarks associated with Manhanset Manor were vanishing with remarkable rapidity, some by design, some by accident. In 1926 a new golf clubhouse was built, and all related activities were promptly shifted from the Village to the present location, on a hill at the center of the course. Title to about sixteen acres of land containing the tees, greens and fairways was transferred from the Unity Investing Corporation to the now legally incorporated Dering Harbor Golf Club. The course itself was redesigned. These transactions were apparently completed only a year before the death of William T. Barr, the man who had personally made a bid for the golf course at the auction in 1918 and who almost singlehandedly piloted the club through ten of its most difficult years. Soon nature began to reclaim the first tee and eighteenth green, just across from the old Casino. For all practical purposes golf, too, had left the Village.

This was the same year in which the massive "Atha cottage"[7] went up in flames. The fire was reported in a two-column spread on the front page of the Greenport paper. Described as "one of the showplaces of Dering Harbor" and "one of the largest and most modern" cottages on the Island, the rambling structure was only twenty years old. Fire companies from Greenport and Sag Harbor came to the assistance of the Shelter Island brigade, the Greenport pumper remaining on a ferry tied to Poor's dock at the foot of the street. But the frame building was soon beyond hope and all efforts were applied to saving nearby cottages, some of which were already badly blistered and scorched. Fortunately there was no wind. Cause of fire? A kerosene hot water heater in the kitchen had exploded.[8]

That spectacular blaze left a yawning gap in the line of houses across from the gate posts leading to Poor's Point, and set off a chain of events that completely altered the profile of old Patchogue Avenue. Always concerned for the protection of the Village and his investment in it, Professor Poor bought the empty lot. He was already in possession of the former guest cottage to the east of it, and two years later he was able to secure the cottage to the west as well. Thereupon he commissioned his son, Alfred Easton Poor, to transform this last acquisition both inside and out. The Victorian disappeared and a Greek Revival house emerged! Other commissions followed for the young architect, including the Carroll cottage and the Village hall. Then he turned his attention to his father's earlier purchase. Thus both of the Poor rental cottages received handsome new façades, embellished with fine old front doors from Greenport. Their new names—Eastgate and Westgate—described their location across from Poor's driveway. The architect's work had given Locust Point a gracious neo-classical stamp.

On Keeping the Trustees Busy

The 1920s were years of frenetic land development all along the hitherto untouched shores of Shelter Island. The Chamber of Commerce had been extremely active. Both the Peconic Lodge, begun as a camp for girls, and the Pridwin Hotel on Crescent Beach, date to this period. But the most far-reaching projects bracketed Coecles Harbor on the opposite side of the island. Almost simultaneously, two of the largest remaining "unimproved" areas fell into off-island hands. Big and Little Ram Islands were sold to James W. Gerard, a former U. S. Ambassador to Germany, who immediately resold them to developers. This duplex peninsula, which had been in the possession of one family, the Tuthills, for two centuries, was to be carefully transformed into a private community with gateposts and guards. Steam shovels arrived to build up the causeway,[2] lots were sold and in two years the first house was ready for occupancy.

The other major transaction was the sale of the Nicholl estate—Mashomack's 2,200 acres—to the banker Otto H. Kahn, apparently with the thought of similar development, but nothing happened.[10] A year later, in 1927, Hilo Shores above West Neck Harbor was launched by Stephen Baldwin for people of "moderate means." He was a prominent and well-to-do lawyer from New York City, the father of novelist Faith Baldwin, who spent many of her early summers and wrote some of her first stories on the Island.

So far as Dering Harbor was concerned, it had appeared—for a while at least—that the losses of the year 1926 might be canceled out by the development of the unimproved woodland between "Germantown" and Dinah's Rock. Several acres fronting on the channel had been bought by a Captain Ernest Lucas or his daughter, Mrs. Alford, with the announced intention of erecting a cottage. As time passed, however, nothing happened except for the sale of a part of the tract to another family with the professed purpose of building upon it. Then came the crash of 1929.

Meanwhile, a "mini-development" of another sort, in the heart of the Village, was proposed but blocked by the Board of Trustees. The planner, who used up a good deal of the trustees' time and most of the mayor's patience, was a well-to-do Bronx merchant named Alfred M. Rogers. To him must go the credit for reuniting the former Casino and its ill-starred annex by purchasing the former from the Triton Investing Company and the latter from the estate of Artemas Ward.[11] His aim was to convert the annex into a community garage for about ten cars, with living quarters if desired, for chauffeurs. He also expected, while occupying the main house, to build guest cottages for other members of his family. At least that is what the mayor conveyed in a letter to the Village counsel. The Board had vetoed these proposals before Black Friday in 1929 could do so, and many private chauffeurs presumably lost their jobs. Considerable renovation was undertaken in any event, the annex being reduced by a good third to make it more compatible in size and shape with the main building.

Endless conflicts seemed to accompany Rogers' tenancy. Whether or not he was altogether to blame is far from clear. The trustees charged him, variously, with "offensive odors" emanating from fires on his beach, with improper maintenance of the roadside property, and even with the surreptitious removal of boundary markers. The major bone of contention was the boundary line between himself and Professor Poor. Both men claimed title to the whole of the old road leading down to the former wharf. The case was eventually taken to court and Poor won. Not long afterward Rogers sold out and left Dering Harbor. A subsequent effort was made by the Town authorities to claim the same road for a town landing; but owing to the statute of limitation as well as Poor's determined resistance, nothing came of it. He was a fighter.

In his capacity as professor of celestial mechanics at Columbia University, Mayor Poor, in a paper presented to the American Association for the Advancement of Science at Philadelphia in 1927, mounted a sustained attack on Albert Einstein charging the great physicist with mathematical error in the practical application of his theories in the deflection of light. According to reports in the *Philadelphia Record*, reprinted on February 5 in the respected *Literary Digest*, Professor Poor's critique found "a sympathetic audience" and "not one of the astronomers present defended Einstein in his views."

Two years later, the *Brooklyn Daily Eagle's* front page carried a headline: "Downfall of Relativity Due to Lack of Evidence Predicted by Professor Poor." The crucial sentences read: "The reign of relativity is rapidly coming to a close as it reaches the tenth anniversary of its first flush of publicity. The theory is based on known error which has never been corrected." The article describes Professor Poor as "adequately provided with the intellectual equipment that permits him to wade with ease through the mathematical profundities that have been published by workers in the relativity field."

Further research may uncover a reply by Einstein to Poor's attack. So far as local history is concerned, one can only marvel at the range and depth of the Mayor's jealous interests, from his miniscule village to the outer reaches of the universe.

The Heatherton Trophy

The only construction in the Village between the two world wars, aside from a rash of private garages and a dock or two, came shortly before the great crash. It involved the razing of two old cottages and the building of three new ones. As we have seen, the younger Towl brothers, Allan and Burr, were responsible for two of these projects. Burr Towl built his from scratch on Locust Point Road; Allan first razed the 40-year-old Putnam place, then spread his new house over two lots facing the harbor.[12]

Also destined to disappear was the Bateman cottage, another well-known landmark of the 1880s. Its new owner, who lived next door, was probably the most strongly defined personality of this decade, always excepting the mayor himself.

James W. Heatherton had come over from the Heights in 1922 and bought the large cottage that had supposedly been occupied by Minnie Maddern Fiske.[13] A man of small stature and Napoleonic propensities, Heatherton gave his name to the trophies awarded annually by the Shelter Island Yacht Club, of which he was a very active member and quondam commodore. For him, to be a member of anything was to be active! His commercial letterhead underwent several changes but his affluence seems to have been derived principally from *The Plumbers* Trade Journal*, which he founded in 1881, and various real estate enterprises. On Shelter Island for instance, he developed The Hedges, a cluster of small cottages just off the North Ferry Road.

No sooner had he taken possession of his new purchase from the original owner, John L. Luning, than he completely renovated it to what was declared "the most modern and picturesque building on the Island by those who accepted his invitation to look it over."[14] At the same time he girdled the whole property with a brick wall, erected a large garage and—a year later still going strong—bought the frame cottage that had been built next door forty years before by the surveyor C. H. Bateman. This he tore down and in its place he put up a conventional brick and stucco house.[15]

Just why he chose to incur so much additional expense is far from clear. According to one hypothesis, the Bateman house was not particularly attractive, especially after twenty-five years of rental to different and indifferent tenants. Perhaps Heatherton viewed it as a possible nuisance or even a threat to the value of his property. Or perhaps Mrs. Bateman was simply eager to unload. A second hypothesis is that Heatherton acquired the property in order to offer a new cottage to his good friends Harry and Nell Prudden and their two attractive daughters. Prudden, a publisher's representative, owned and occupied the house for about twelve years, but whether he ever paid for it or, if so, how much, remains in question. He even had a hard time buying up the adjacent shorefront when the Village offered it for sale at $400. By 1937 financial problems forced him to relinquish the cottage altogether, whereupon Heatherton's real estate firm took title to it.

In an effort to merge the two properties, Heatherton then petitioned the trustees for permission to close the street between his two houses, while insisting that the overgrown Yoco Avenue on his southern flank be properly opened up. The numerous letters he fired at the Village board complained, among other things, that the local current was not powerful enough to run his electric piano and movie "projectoscope." He and the authorities engaged in repeated skirmishes over who was responsible for the maintenance of Yoco Avenue—though, strangely enough, many years elapsed before the Village made the belated charge that the Heatherton brick walls, coming to the very edge of Shore Road, encroached on the public right of way.

Nor was the Heathertons' family life exactly placid. During a contentious divorce proceeding Mrs. Heatherton laid claim to the Dering Harbor house, but her husband ultimately retained possession of it. Shortly thereafter he married his much younger niece and former ward, to the wagging of many tongues.

Whether or not the difficulties between the Village board and cottage owners such as Rogers and Heatherton could have been avoided by prior adoption of a building code and zoning ordinances is somewhat problematical. A draft proposal along these lines, which would have become Ordinance #2, was discussed in 1928 at an inconclusive public hearing attended by twenty-five persons. A couple of months later, when most of the cottages had been closed for the season, the trustees put into effect a policy statement entitled "Building Rules and Regulations." Sidestepping #2 entirely, the next ordinance mentioned in the minutes, placing parking restrictions on motor vehicles, is tagged #3 !

Flaming Crosses—and at Last, a Fire Engine

The Village and its people reflected the times in which they lived. The era following World War I was a turbulent one. Maybe this was the reason why Dering Harbor did not seem to miss the excitement of the big hotel. A few nationally known figures visited the Island as heretofore. Some including "Mrs. ex-President Tyler," being a Gardiner, stayed at Sylvester Manor. Others such as James Fenimore Cooper came over from Sag Harbor to visit the Nicholls.[16] But the parade of distinguished guests in and out of Manhanset's famous watering place had stopped. Among the many tenants of cottages during this decade, the most noteworthy seems to have been the Spanish consul from New York City, Señor Luis Llanso, who regularly filled the Cartwright cottage with his fourteen very well-behaved children.

From their vantage point along the shore the Llanso family no doubt saw the flaming crosses that were occasionally set alight on Sunset Rock by zealous adherents of the Ku Klux Klan. They could also listen to the daily gossip about rum-runners who plied the waters of eastern Long Island at night to unload their illicit cargo. They no doubt worried for their brood of children when Camp Quinipet closed down tight in midsummer and abruptly sent home 250 boys, some by special train, to forestall an epidemic of German measles.

Despite alarums and excursions, the little Village found itself in condition to weather the heavy seas of the great depression which was to hit the nation with full force in the 1930s. In fact, the time seemed precisely right to proceed with two major building projects—or, more accurately, with a single "master plan" in two stages, the second of which was to be a stately Village hall.

The first stage was designed to consolidate all Village services within the maintenance area where the water tank and well, the power plant and incinerator were already located. Provision had to be made to accommodate both superintendent Joseph Mawrey's family and a second-hand pumper which the trustees were planning to buy in the following year. These two major housing requirements were met, thriftily it seems, by remodeling the former hotel laundry adjoining the power house. Without removing the last of the wash tubs still lining the walls, the ground floor became the firehouse and the upper story became the superintendent's residence, all at an allocated cost of $12,500.

Polly Mawrey, who grew up as "the only child in Dering Harbor," retained clear memories of "the Ahrens-Fox firetruck that dominated our lives." Consecutive blazes had left a trail of scars on the memory of summer residents. Two years before the terrible Atha fire, the Bancroft cottage had been threatened with destruction by the explosion of an oil stove,[17] and more recently Mayor Poor's 54-foot launch *Myra* had caught fire on the way to Greenport.[18] Consequently Joseph Mawrey was in a state of constant alert, not only to protect the little village but to answer alarms anywhere on the Island, including the memorable fire when it burned down Prospect Hotel in 1942.

"The tension and responsibility caused by the presence of the fire truck overshadowed my parents' lives for twenty years," Polly Mawrey recalls. "It was always there—24 hours a day, 364 days a year.... No one else lived very close and not many could or would take responsibility for getting the truck to a fire.

At its peak the volunteer unit attached to the village engine numbered fourteen men. A snapshot shows them standing at attention in their white uniforms under a large Dering Harbor banner draped over the fire truck. In the absence of other excitement, little Polly enjoyed watching the fire drills or helping her father with his seasonal chores, such as flushing out the water hydrants, checking the street lamps or just cycling around the "hibernating village" to see that all was well. Occasionally, father and daughter "performed impromptu tapdances on the spacious wooden verandas," and once they came upon a small whale washed up on shore.

When World War II broke out, the eight-year-old girl, whose bedroom window overlooked the unglamorous incinerator, found in the firetruck "a magnificent toy." Hearing about air battles and bombings, "I would climb into the cockpit of my bomber, check the array of gauges, glance back at the gun turret [ie., hose reel] to make sure all was in order and then I was 'airborne.' "

All in all, the new house, with its ground floor almost totally preempted by the fire engine, seems to have served its purpose well—putting a prompt stop to all major fires in the village from that day to this!

S. Gustafson

Chapter VIII

FROM VILLAGE HALL
TO HURRICANE
1930-40

THE PROPOSAL to build a new Village Hall, if the Board minutes can be given full credence, was sparked by the desirability of having a fireproof vault for the official records. Such a storage place was, it seemed, a requirement of state law. Whether or not a large safe could satisfy the legal requirement may have been discussed, but probably not at great length. Now that a decade had been devoted to toning up all the nerves and sinews of public service, the time had come to do something about the public image of the little Village. A hand-me-down hall—actually a converted cottage—did not accord with Mayor Poor's highly developed sense of the fitness of things, as revealed in the houses he had built or remodeled and the Casino he had espoused.

Strangely enough, given the times, there seems to have been no violent opposition to the idea. Either the depression had not affected the villagers or they felt impervious to it—as yet. At a public hearing, the relative merits of remodeling the existing structure and of building a new one were debated.[1] The matter of location was also broached and there was some unimaginative sentiment in favor of clustering all facilities in the immediate vicinity of the water tower and power plant—that is, on a less valuable site so that the present lot could be sold to good advantage, presumably for another handsome cottage.

The upshot of the open meeting, however, was a general agreement to retain the site along the main road but not to try to remodel the old building, already dilapidated at the time of its purchase for $2,550 twelve years before. Having once housed various busy offices related to behind-the-scenes operations at the big hotel, it now bore all the scars of a half century's hard use. One letter credits the omnipresent Thomas Wood with having constructed it as a private dwelling in the earliest years of Shelter Island Park—and this, in view of its central location, could be correct.[2] For a while the thrifty trustees considered the feasibility of moving the house back to the utilities area as a staff residence, but, as we have seen, the idea was dropped in favor of converting an already existing building to that purpose, using only as much of the plumbing fixtures and other equipment as could readily be salvaged.[3]

Once the preliminary decisions had been taken, plans for the new civic center made rapid progress. A Village architect had been officially appointed two years earlier.[4] This was Alfred Easton Poor who, on the threshold of a long and distinguished career in his profession, had already demonstrated his talent in the successful renovation of Westgate and of the Carroll cottage. A ceiling cost of $15,000 was put upon the new hall, but the bid came to only $13,000. The architect's fee was $600.[5]

Further shifts of boundary lines, including the elimination of the alley, were undertaken so that the new structure would have a proper fronting on Locust Point Avenue, flanked by two residential streets. The modest concept of a "suitable hall and clerk's office" was expanded to include a board room. A very elaborate landscaping proposal was drawn up but considerably modified for budgetary reasons. The first furnishings were loaned by the Poors, with an option to buy at a reasonable figure—an option that was finally exercised nine years later in the amount of $500.

At the formal inauguration of the new center (followed by refreshments) on September 12, 1931, Mayor Poor, in a three-page address, reviewed the achievements of the past fifteen years. He also sounded a note of warning on "danger spots within the village," namely "the nuisances accompanying motor traffic and irresponsible tourists." But, he added, "the trustees hope, before another season, to have the Village safeguarded in every possible way"—no doubt a reference to Ordinance #3, which had just been adopted. It provided for a public parking lot "easterly of the power plant" and restricted the parking of motor cars along the roads to not more than thirty minutes.[6]

The Mayor then concluded: "With these points in mind, I hope and trust that the opening of our new Hall will bring the residents of the Village closer together; that it will provide a meeting place for amusement as well as for serious business. Let us, therefore, dedicate this new building to a better understanding among us all, to a spirit of cooperation in all Village affairs, and to a determination to protect our interests and our property from outside encroachments and from the nuisance of unrestricted motor traffic."

The Village—bereft of hotel, Casino, country club, chapel, bathing beach and even a recreation pier—now had a new hub. At infrequent intervals it became the scene of receptions and other civic events. With these few exceptions, however, its chief function, aside from the fulfilment of bureaucratic necessities, was to serve as the visible symbol of community rather than as the center of social activity. Public funds, needless to say, were not available for parties.

The structural heart of this new communal symbol was a capacious fireproof vault to which the documents and official records of the Village were now confidently entrusted. But it soon became apparent that a little fire is better than none at all, especially when solid ice carpets the channel from Shelter Island to Greenport as it did in 1934. In plain English, no provision had been made heat the headquarters of this summer colony, and dampness now proved as destructive of paper as fire could be—only somewhat slower. So, until a furnace could be installed, there was nothing to do but remove the contents of the vault to a warmer place during the winter months. It was about this time also that a new clerk, Mrs. Helen Loper, was appointed, and she could hardly be expected to work in an unheated office.[7] The situation was corrected in 1936 at a cost of approximately (1,000. There was no further problem until the flow of heating oil stopped during World War II, with considerable damage to the whole building.

The Deepening Depression

Despite the acquisition of a rather impressive center—for so small a community—and the addition of a fire department, the Village trustees remained intent on a cautiously modest, pay-as-you-go policy. The worsening depression reinforced their natural inclination to keep expenses to a minimum—and may also have been to blame for the mean theft of a lead statue from the fountain in the sunken gardens outside the hall. Only a week after the dedication the Board decided, without giving its reason, to "divest" the Village of its beachfront "parks," namely, two small pieces of shorefront at the foot of Yoco Avenue and Dering Lane respectively, by offering them at auction to adjacent property owners.[8]

Thus the entire beachfront, which the first developers had intended to reserve as a public park, now became private property. Of course those early planners had been thinking of a hotel-centered community in which the corporation would continue to exercise all rights and duties with respect to control and maintenance of the shorefront. Perhaps the reason for divestiture may have been the cost of upkeep, although the maintenance of two small plots could hardly amount to very much. A deeper reason no doubt lay in Professor Poor's stated contention that the hotel corporation of twenty years before had been misguided in refusing to sell shorefront property to prospective cottage-builders. Consequently, when Island Realty superseded the bankrupt Manhanset Improvement Corporation after the second fire, the original policy was revised and beach tracts were systematically sold off to owners of adjacent cottages. Professor Poor himself had long since acquired all the shorefront land from the former bathing beach to the old hotel wharf—in other words, Locust Point had become Poor's Point. Title to the foot-of-street shorefront at Gardiner Way seems to have been included in the Allan Towl purchase, with the

J. P. Morgan in Dering Harbor, at the helm of his *Corsair*
The ship's bell is now a feature of the Morgan Library in Manhattan

Old Oak still standing on Upper Shore Road

Lawn Tennis at rear of New Manhanset House, circa 1904

informal understanding that the cottage owners along that street would share in both the use and the expense of the dock. This understanding lingered in effect for many years, then languished and was finally extinguished in a simple letter from the new owner when the property was sold after Mr. Towl's death in 1967.[9]

While the liquidation of the public parks was being accomplished, a much larger issue commanded the attention of the whole of eastern Long Island. This was a strong movement to link the North and South Forks by a bridge traversing Shelter Island. Surveys had been made and the project was in the early planning stages, although far from being finally approved. It was foreseen that footings for the North Fork span would probably land within the Village.

Mayor Poor gave the matter his usual prompt and energetic attention, and the trustees soon registered a strong official protest against the erection of any bridge, using technical arguments regarding its adverse effect on water traffic, especially sailing vessels, in the channel narrows. This opposition ran counter to the strong support given the project by local newspapers and business interests, who equated speed of transportation with progress. The debate continued for several years. One of Mayor Poor's letters, containing an analysis of prohibitive costs, was given first-page space by the *Suffolk Weekly Times*[10]— which, however, cheered wholeheartedly when WPA funds were budgeted for the project a few months later. Happily for Mayor Poor and the Village, the proposal foundered.

The climate of the 1930s was not auspicious for undertaking fresh ventures, locally or elsewhere. Most Villagers personally had no wish to assume new obligations or responsibilities; some were in fact eager to sell out, though not at an extreme loss; still others were holding on to their summer homes, by their fingernails, so to speak. In June 1930 it was publicly noted that "three of the finest properties in Dering Harbor" were up for sale.[11] A year later, the purchase of one of the gingerbread cottages was heralded as "one of the most important real estate transactions" for some time.[12] A bit later the brother of one of the "Germantown" group, himself a frequent visitor to Dering Harbor, committed suicide.[13] The financial crisis deepened and as late as 1935 the Village clerk observed in a letter that "last season several cottages were closed and, at times, the Village looked quite deserted." One welcome "windfall" in that year was an item of $4.25 accruing to the state's smallest Village as its proportionate (39 residents) share of revenue collected by the state on the sale of alcoholic beverages.[14]

A generally bleak situation was plainly reflected in the unusually large number of rentals, as well as in the extra effort required to collect taxes.

Repeated warnings to property owners of possible tax sale became numerous. In a classic instance, the director of a well-known firm had bought and improved one of the older cottages during the mid-1920s, only to lose his job when the company went bankrupt. From then on, even after he landed another position, it was touch and go as to whether the cottage could be rented for a month or more each summer in order to pay taxes and avoid public sale. Tenaciously, he held onto the house for twenty years.

Five of the six houses on Gardiner Way, for example, were regularly for rent from approximately the mid-1930's to the mid-1940s. Most of the lessees, so far as the names are known, seem to have come from New York City or northern New Jersey, rarely for more than one or two seasons. The only conspicuously "droppable" names were those of Norman bel Geddes and his daughter Barbara, who occupied one of the gingerbread cottages for two years.[15] Not until after World War II did a new trend set in, as these income-producing cottages were gradually bought up by other people for use as summer homes.

No account of these depression years should ignore mention of an open letter from the Mayor of Dering Harbor—as an outraged citizen—to the President of the United States. It was defiantly dated July 4, 1934. Not long before F.D.R. had addressed the nation confidently inviting his fellow Americans to consider whether they were not better off than a year earlier.

To this invitation, Poor replied with a thundering No. "You and your administration," he wrote, "have cut my savings more than in half: you have destroyed at least 60% of the former value of my property." He went on to berate the President for establishing the Tennessee Valley Authority "to compete with existing plants and... to wreck the investment values of bonds and stocks of many companies." He also chastised F.D.R. for abandoning the gold standard, establishing a federal agency over radio "to stifle all criticism of your acts and policies," for subsidizing various agricultural products, for openly threatening "to step on the toes of special privilege," and for classifying critics ("us") as doubting Thomases!

Mr. Hench Administers Oxygen, So to Speak

But it was in this same difficult decade that attention in the Village turned toward a pair of hitherto undeveloped areas. One was the acreage between "Germantown" and Dinah's Rock; the other was the wooded upland that had once concealed the outbuildings of the hotel and that later became, for some years, a part of the golf course. Only one private cottage had ever been built within the loop formed by the two main arteries of traffic through the Village, Locust Point Road and Manhanset Road—the Burr Towl house, built a few years earlier. Indeed[16], with the possible exception of the two converted carriage houses on South Street, the statement still obtains.

La Verne Hench came to the Village with some fresh and constructive ideas, as well as the means to implement them. Originally from Ohio, the Henches lived in South Orange. He was head of the American Oxygen Service in Harrison, New Jersey. It happened that his family and the Carrolls employed the same piano teacher in New Jersey. As a result of this harmonious acquaintance, the Henches rented the Carroll cottage for three summers. Which leads to the Carrolls themselves.

Stephen Carroll was a law school graduate who in the course of a business career had founded the Heat and Cold Equipment Company of Paterson, New Jersey, become the first representative of the General Electric Company in that state and later, during World War II, operated two hotels for service men in Paterson. In 1928 he had bought the Cartwright cottage along with its tangible and intangible mementos of Mrs. Leslie Carter and David Belasco, and immediately engaged Alfred Easton Poor to redesign it. Nothing was lost and much was gained in this process, since the personality of the old house, judging from existing photographs, did not begin to match that of the glamorous Mrs. Carter. The young architect pushed the nondescript and middle-aged building back uphill from the Shore Road, gave it a quarter turn, and by the addition of tall white columns transformed the dowdy structure into the likeness of a gracious Southern mansion. As Professor Poor proudly wrote to Forrest Towl, the result was "now one of the best houses in the Village."[17] This, then, had been the house in which the Henches first summered.

At the death of Adolf Kuttroff in 1936 the "Germantown" cottage he had built more than forty years before came on the market.[18] Mr. Hench bought it and, following the Carrolls * example, thoroughly remodeled it inside and out. It too was moved back, then faced with brick and adorned with Southern colonial porticos. Inside it was renovated literally from top to bottom. As soon as the third floor was finished, the family moved into the future servants' quarters, moving downstairs in stages as the work progressed. Eventually the rejuvenation was complete, including a full-fledged soda fountain in the butler's pantry for the young daughter Alice and the new name of Sunny Ledge.

Massive old boxwood trees planted on either side of the front entrance looked Janus-like to both past and future. Once they had grown at Sylvester Manor; then they had been uprooted and taken to Southold. Now they were returned to Shelter Island to stand guard at Dering Harbor over the home of the young woman who, as Mrs. Andrew Fiske, was later to become lady of Sylvester Manor.

The acquisition of the Kuttroff property was only the first of a series which continued at fairly regular intervals for the next few years, enabling La Verne Hench to give further rein to his various interests and keep the Village trustees busy with a steady stream of applications or petitions for an enlargement of his dock, the construction of a large greenhouse, and the erection of a hydroplane hangar, among other projects.

From the estate of W. P. Pickhardt, Mr. Hench acquired two parcels: the Yoco Avenue beachfront and about nineteen acres of land that had formerly been part either of the golf course or of the undisturbed forest. Here the new owner proceeded to develop a fine tree nursery and arboretum—vestiges of which are still clearly visible behind the handsome beech hedge across from the entrance to the present golf course. An old barn was torn down and the proposed greenhouse was erected in its place. The only person to feel a personal loss at these changes was the superintendent's daughter Polly, who "missed the stately trees and peacefulness of the forest," even though "the greenhouse was soon filled with lovely plants."

The Beginning of Land's End and the Hydroplane Hangar

By 1941 the large estate just east of the Kuttroff place came on the market. It too falls within the scope of the Hench story along with the hydroplane hangar but first another brief digression is called for. The whole area lying between "Germaniown" and Dinah's Rock has been known as Land's End ever since Mr. Hench was asked by a previous owner to suggest a suitable name for it. With the possible exception of a small bungalow, and despite the expressed intentions of Captain Lucas, this tract of a dozen or so acres had remained "unimproved."

The first resident owner seems to have been Mrs. Catherine Lyons—who, according to available tax records, owned a large part of the total acreage, on which there was a pair of bungalows. These were officially distinguished by numbers rather than names. No. 1 included a garage. It was Mrs. Lyons who engaged Alfred Easton Poor in 1930 to build a large brick house. The architect was not in sympathy with her preference for the Tudor style and remembers her as a very difficult person to please. This was to be, with one exception, the last new house erected in Dering Harbor for the next thirty-five years. That single exception was to be a small house inserted unobtrusively along the shore between the Lyons' house and Dinah's Rock.

Within three years Mrs. Lyons sold the property to her good friend and companion Miss Bertha Low, likewise from Morristown, New Jersey, who subsequently acquired the remainder of Land's End, together with another bungalow which became No. 3. As chatelaine of a considerable estate, Miss

Low assigned one cottage to the cook and another, with garage, to her driver; the third, by the tennis court, was known as the playhouse and dance studio. A chain was hung across the gateposts to the large estate, until Miss Low was faced with the option of lowering the barrier or dispensing with the services of the fire department if needed.

Shortly after Miss Low's death in 1940, Mr. Hench was able to buy Land's End from the person to whom it had been bequeathed. According to Mayor Poor, who had a keen eye for such things, the selling price was "one-fifth of its real value." The later subdivision of the estate took place in the following decade and it therefore belongs to the next chapter. Suffice it to say just here that Mr. Hench was now in possession of two ideal landing places for a hydroplane, one near Dinah's Rock on Greenport channel, the other at the foot of Yoco Avenue on Dering Harbor. He thus anticipated by thirty years the use to which the latter site would be put by Mayor Wilcox in his seaplane nights to and from Manhattan.

Just when Mr. Hench first thought of establishing a hydroplane station in Dering Harbor is not known. One July 4 weekend a few years earlier a quartet of hydroplanes had visited the Prospect beach, offering short flights for a modest fee. At about the same time a first effort was made to base an aero-taxi service on the Island, using a Waco *Wasp*, but apparently nothing came of the venture. In any event, when Mr. Hench submitted his application to build a hangar on his "agricultural and farming land," the trustees turned him down.

In 1946, soon after the end of World War II, the famous comedian Ed Wynn descended upon Shelter Island to solicit patrons for a regular air service to Wall Street, using a seven-passenger plane. Mr. Hench was among the first subscribers. A few months later the Long Island Air Lines began constructing a seaplane base with a passenger lounge at Louis's, or Crescent, Beach; here a twelve-passenger Grumman *Mallard* was to land.[19] The band leader Guy Lombardo was reported to have a major financial interest in the enterprise. No regular daily service to New York eventuated however, and after two desultory seasons all these efforts were quietly abandoned. The concrete ramp is still in existence.

Even without the hydroplane hangar, Mr. Hench now had a very big stake in the Village of Dering Harbor. A couple of years earlier he had bought the Pickhardt place, just two doors away from Sunny Ledge, for his daughter Alice and her husband. With the acquisition of all these properties, stretching from the Yoco "beachhead" on Dering Harbor across the abandoned end of the old golf course to the two large Germantown cottages, then including all of Land's End down to Dinah's Rock, Mr. Hench unquestionably had become a leading citizen not only of the Village but of the Island.

The Hurricane of 1938

The economic storms with which the 1930s began were soon succeeded by meteorological disturbances. A blizzard in February 1934, was the worst since 1888, and again the channel froze over. In November 1935 came a 60-m.p.h. "easterly gale" which turned Greenport itself into an island and overturned a Long Island Railroad train on the flooded tracks between Greenport and Southold. At Dering Harbor, according to the village clerk's report to Mayor Poor, "the storm did some damage to practically every property owner on the waterfront... it probably washed some of your bank away, as the wind and the tide was the worst I have ever seen while I have lived here." During the opening weeks of 1936 Shelter Island was icebound for a month and received essential supplies—including bread—by courtesy of the U. S. Coast Guard.

But the real "blockbuster" arrived at the end of the 1938 season—a tropical storm which devastated large sections of eastern Long Island. Winds up to 100 m.p.h. were registered in Greenport, where the list of damaged buildings read like a business directory and the tree-lined streets were stripped of some seven hundred tall elms. One well-known citizen of Shelter Island, Captain Leroy Griffing, drowned in Long Island Sound; otherwise there were no major casualties. The physical destruction, however, was grievous, especially to the woods which so beautifully bordered the roads and clothed the rolling hills.

As the hurricane increased in fury, the Mawrey family gathered food and blankets and took refuge in a small building beyond the range of falling trees and of the tall smokestack that loomed over the supervisor's house. As Polly remembers it, "We were isolated for weeks because of the trees lying across the road. The electric and telephone lines were down all over the area. My father walked to the Heights for groceries once or twice and we sat in the evenings around the kitchen table with only a kerosene lamp for light." But there was water. No sooner had the storm ended than her father removed the flooring over the pit in which the "old Nova gas water pump" lay dormant, and succeeded in reviving it into useful service.

Mayor Poor, whom Polly remembers as a "mysterious, authoritative figure," soon mailed a full report of the report of the storm to all the property owners. It eloquently describes both the havoc of that terrible Wednesday and the prompt measures that restored the stricken Village to something like a functioning unit in a matter of days.

The hurricane of September 21, 1938, wrecked telephone and electric light service, made the roads temporarily impassable, and damaged two water mains... The loss of many large oak trees on the roads and private properties is irreparable...

The electric pumps were put out of use but within one hour after the end of the storm the auxiliary pumps were in working order and water was being pumped in the mains. [Then] breaks were found and it was necessary to cut out two sections of the Village. One serious break was repaired in twelve hours, the others within twenty-four hours.

The auxiliary pumps gave sufficient water for ordinary use... not for fire protection. With the reserve in the tank these pumps might keep a fire engine supplied for about one hour, but no longer. For this reason... bonfires were temporarily prohibited.

"With all wires down," according to the same letter, serious consideration was given to replacing them underground but the estimated cost was too great. For the time being the telephone company threaded temporary lines through the trees, then within ten days replaced all the poles. It took the Shelter Island Light and Power Company twice as long to replace certain essential wires, leaving the eastern cottages still without electricity. Mayor Poor concludes:

The street lighting system was wrecked and it will not be possible to resume service before next season... With the effective assistance of several of the property owners a passage way for automobiles was opened to Shelter Island Heights within about twenty-four hours after the storm. Arrangements were made with the Griffing Brothers to cut the large trees obstructing the highways, and, with the aid of their tractor, the main highway and the Shore Road were cleared within a few days. The work of clearing Manhanset Road through the woods was too heavy for the Village force, and arrangements were made with the Town Superintendent of Highways to do this work at the cost of the Village. Extra men have been hired and the work of clearing the roadsides is being slowly carried out.

The cost to the Village of clearing and repairing the roads, of rewiring the lighting system, and of revamping the street lights will be heavy. Fortunately, however, the Village has a cash surplus on hand which, with the balance of taxes due in March, should be sufficient to meet these costs. But all surpluses, in the various departments and in the general funds, will be wiped out. No additional taxes now seem to be necessary ; but no tax reduction can be expected.

In its own way the century's third decade had indeed been a memorable if not an altogether happy one. Whether Dale Carnegie's visits about this time—he stopped at Sylvan Lodge on his fishing holidays—had any effect one way or the other is not known. Those who prefer to look only on the bright side of things could, of course, point out that the big bridges from the North and South Forks were *not* built. Those who prefer to fear the worst could console themselves with the thought that if the bridges had been built, the hurricane might—on an ill-wind-that-blows-no-good basis-have blown them down! Without casualties, of course.

Chapter IX

THE REPERCUSSIONS OF WAR
1940-60

BY 1940 the thirty households in Dering Harbor were well on their way to becoming an authentic political community consisting entirely of "summer" residents. Several decades of semi-parasitical dependence on a famous resort hotel had been followed by two decades of self-government, and the village had learned to shift for itself. It had weathered successively the loss of the glamorous Manhanset House, the dissolution of its short-lived country club, the dislocations of World War I, the withdrawal of its golf course, and the Wall Street crash. Now, as it slowly recovered from the shattering blow of the 1938 hurricane, World War II exploded.

But while large areas of the world felt the full impact of the Wagnerian storm which raged first in Europe, then spread to many corners of the globe, the conflict barely lapped the Island-sheltered-by-islands. The word "lapped" is deliberately chosen. Actual hostilities never came closer than Amagansett, where one night in June 1942 eight German saboteurs scrambled ashore with a good supply of high explosives and $150,000 in cash. They were rounded up, ingloriously, within a week.[1] Except for those Islanders who joined up and moved out, the war otherwise remained a distant event. The incident at Amagansett served only to encourage participation in the war effort and in civil defense.

The first Island-wide trial blackout, conducted even before the U. S. entered the war, had been "carried out with great efficiency." Flares simulated firebombs, Disch's drugstore was "hit" and all emergency equipment was orchestrated to handle the mock attack.[2] Then came Pearl Harbor. While Greenport was inviting all her citizens to cooperate in a common effort to place buckets of sand at strategic locations—on street corners, in stairwells, etc.—in the event of an air raid, the following report came from across the channel:

"Shelter Island responded to the national crisis last week with calm and efficiency. The Civil Defense Council immediately established a 24-hour schedule and a 24-hour watch was maintained at the observation post at Walter King's home. So far the watchers have paced back and forth in the King dooryard, their chill vigils somewhat lightened by black coffee and tasty dishes sent in by the women of the Island."[3]

The first watch tower was built in the Walter Kings' dooryard; a year later,

First Village Fire Engine and Polly Mawrey, Superintendent's Daughter

New Village Hall, dedicated 1931. Photograph by Scott Harris

Ex-Mayor George Genung with Mrs. Genung at Centennial Picknick, 1974. Photograph by Scott Harris

a new one was erected on the brick wing of the schoolhouse. Quite a different matter from the observation tower built on White Hill years before for enjoyment of the panoramic view! As the war wore on, enthusiasm wore off. Pleas for sky-scanners became more desperate. Finally, with the approach of another long, cold winter, General "Hap" Arnold officially reduced the 24-hour vigil to "intervals," whereupon Shelter Island limited its watch to Wednesday afternoons.[4]

Other protective measures were, of course, drastically enforced. Lights were dimmed all along the eastern seaboard. Gasoline was rationed, later all pleasure driving forbidden. The honor roll of young Islanders in military service grew steadily longer. Greenport churned out minesweepers, with frequent encouragement from celebrities such as Lily Pons and Kate Smith who came to launch them. Belts were tightened. Local fishermen found a commercial market even for blowfish and sea robins.

Side effects took many forms. The fairways of the Dering Harbor Golf Club reverted to the production of food. In a certain sense, the New Prospect House also became a casualty of war. After the seventy-year-old hotel suddenly burned down just before the 1942 season opened wartime restrictions were among the reasons for not rebuilding it. In fact, it was uneconomical to do so. For Shelter Island, the era of the great seaside resort was definitely past. Less pretentious and more intimate hotels took over.

The hotel-less Village of Dering Harbor was affected primarily by fuel rationing. As was inevitable, all the summer homes suffered from various degrees of neglect. A time of enforced shabbiness set in. Vacation resorts, after all, could hardly expect to enjoy special consideration in the midst of the war effort. Thirty gallons of gasoline had to suffice for the truck during the summer and in winter there was no heating oil for the hall and its fireproof vault. By 1943 the roof was leaking—just as, ironically, a new and deeper well had to be dug to improve the water supply! Moisture severely damaged the ceilings, walls and floors of the rooms.

The deteriorating hall nevertheless made its positive patriotic contribution. As many as a dozen ladies, led by the mayor's wife, gathered twice weekly during the summer season to prepare thousands of surgical dressings for Halloran Hospital on Staten Island.[5] Mr. Heatherton—and no doubt other yachtsmen along with Mayor Poor—loaned their pleasure craft to the Coast Guard "for the duration."[6]

The Village owed its survival under these adverse conditions not so much to its autonomy as to the basic stability and loyalty of the individual property owners. Little by little all vestiges of the depression had disappeared under a rising tide of wartime prosperity, until by 1947 the Trustees were able to pay off all remaining indebtedness. But above all, this solvency was due to the deep-rooted tenacity—in many instances spanning the two world wars—of Dering

Harbor residents in holding on to their summer homes. During the previous half century, more than a score of families had retained and maintained their cottages for at least twenty-five years!

Professor and Mrs. Poor held the record: sixty years of continuous summer residence, not counting the summers they had spent at the Manhanset House. The three Towl brothers amassed a combined total of 122 years—the shortest span being thirty-six years aside from several previous summers in the Heights. Several other owners approached or passed the forty-year milestone. This pattern of longevity still obtains and continues to contribute to the steadiness of the Village; thus, a majority of the houses that changed hands during the 1940s remain with the same owners today.[7]

This tribute to stability having been paid, it must be observed that the incidence of departures and arrivals in the decade of the World War II was exceptionally high. Wars are notorious for their unsettling effect on individuals and communities. Established patterns and habits are disrupted; values shift. The cost of labor and essential commodities tends to rise; prices of non-essentials such as summer homes, meanwhile, may fall. As we have already seen, the large estate known as Land's End was sold at the beginning of the war for considerably less than its original cost.

How things would have turned out if there had been no war is impossible to say, but the twelve acres of land with numerous buildings were destined to be split up; the times were not propitious for disposing advantageously of a large country estate requiring a retinue of servants. So, in 1942, the big English Tudor house was sold, minus its appendages, to Dr. Walter Lundblad, a son-in-law of J. W. Heatherton. Mr. Hench retained the tennis court for his daughter Alice, and assigned one of the cottages with its five-car garage to the family chauffeur.[8] Part of that garage has since become a large living room.

While the cook's cottage in the far corner of the estate remained undisturbed, various other structures were ingeniously amalgamated into an attractive new cottage. After selling the big house, Mr. Hench found himself with an orphaned assortment of small buildings. These he consolidated, allegedly with the architectural counsel of Alfred Easton Poor, into a family-sized bungalow. The procedure appears have been somewhat as follows.

To a new site, near the eastern edge of the property, he moved the party pavilion that had stood close to the tennis court. It would serve admirably as a living room. Beside it he established a square wooden tower that had stood near the beach, apparently as a bathhouse. At the new location its ground floor became a kitchen and its second floor an airy bedroom with enormous windows. Two other wooden buildings of undetermined origin were coopted to provide additional "wings"—and lo, a cottage! To round out the story of this modular house, it should be said that in subsequent years much more has been done— the excavation of a full basement, for example—to transform a seasonal bungalow into a year-round home.[9]

Mayor Poor Retires—And Other Changes

The changes wrought in "Little Germany" were even more startling than those taking place behind the brick gateposts of Land's End. After 1943 only Mrs. Belle Schwarzmann, the daughter-in-law of the man who commissioned Stanford White to design him a house, remained to carry on the name of an original owner-builder. She and her husband were childless and bequeathed their handsome property to Harvard University. It was she who began the process of dismantling Germantown by razing the Lidgerwood cottage next door. At the same time she had an indirect, and perhaps inadvertent, hand in adding a small residence to the village when she sold the former Lidgerwood stable on South Street to Roswell Ward, who turned it into a summer home.[10]

Although it was customary for Dering Harbor wives to hold title to summer cottages, no woman had ever been elected to the Board of Trustees. In all likelihood, World War II helped to dissolve this barrier, just as its predecessor played a decisive role in giving women the right to vote. It will be remembered that the Village could not have been established in 1916 without a unique "loophole" in the law that recognized the distaff ballot in this one instance only! Now, after the death of William Pickhart in 1940, Mrs. Dorothy P. Kahle succeeded her brother and served for several years as a regularly elected trustee. She it was who thoughtfully donated a twelve-cylinder Packard limousine, which became the Town's first ambulance. As such, it was in use from 1946 to 1953. The heavy vehicle, used by her mother, was equipped with special springs and a wheel chair ramp. It had been custom built, according to Mrs. Kahle, for a Mrs. Carter of Carter's Little Liver Pills, who had lived to enjoy it only a few weeks. Its rate of gasoline consumption was four miles per gallon.

The official minutes of the Village Board pay little or no attention to the war against the Axis powers. Monthly agendas confined themselves to the usual details municipal management and citizen complaints—redress of property assessments, for instance. In 1941 the Hall grounds were garlanded with 275 feet of althea hedge at a cost of $110. By 1944 the auditors faulted the Village for spending $20 on a public reception. That same summer, a severe tropical storm vented its fury on the bulwarks along the shore. The next year, shortly after V-E Day, Dr. Prime denied the Village further use of the dump which was on his land, thus causing a temporary crisis.

Two major changes came in 1948. At long last the Village disengaged itself from the contentious electricity business by selling the entire plant to the Shelter Island Light &: Power Company for $4,000, noting for the record that the equipment when new had cost $5,500. Thus the incandescent "torch" which the Manhanset House used to illuminate its public rooms sixty years earlier was transmitted by the Village to the Town and eventually, a dozen years later, to the utility now known as Lilco.

At the annual meeting on July 6, 1948, the mayoral torch also changed hands, for the first time in twenty-nine years. There was no fanfare. Professor Poor in a brief speech welcomed his successor and, in turn, accepted a resolution of gratitude from the whole community.

The third mayor, William O'Conor,. like the first was a lawyer from New York City. He was no newcomer, having bought the first Burr Towl cottage in 1929.[11] His tenure as a resident, thirty-eight years, was much longer than his term of office. He resigned after nine years, pleading prolonged absences in the summer. For two years thereafter the office was filled by Henry G. Carpenter, who then moved to Florida.

An Atom Bomb Attack—Simulated

In the ten years of the O'Conor-Carpenter administration, roughly from 1950 to 1960, the Village seemed to relax, not unlike a small sloop easing gratefully into a snug haven out of high winds and choppy seas. Having Mayor Poor at the helm was, in a sense, like being in the eye of a perpetual minor storm. Fortunately, he was a competent captain—albeit something of a martinet.

Shelter Island itself was continuing to prosper as a result of the postwar boom. The agricultural specialty at the time was lima beans. For nearly twenty-five years the local crop had captured a "good share" of metropolitan New York's market in late summer and early fall. But rising costs—labor, ferry tolls and erratic prices on the auction block in Southold—called for concerted action. As reported in the *Sag Harbor Express*, "Shelter Island farmers have departed from their rugged individualism... and formed a cooperative to insure a steadier market and a decrease in harvesting costs for their principal product."[12] Nearly a dozen men pooled their resources to transform a large garage into a processing and freezing plant.

The predicament of the Shelter Island farmers was one part of a much larger picture. More farm labor was needed to bring in eastern Suffolk County's potato crop, and six hundred jobs were offered to Displaced Persons from the refugee camps of postwar Europe—far more than the International Refugee

Organization seemed able to supply. Only 150 DPs, mostly Polish, had responded to the invitation. A supplementary contingent of seventy arrived by ship—too late for the early harvest in 1950 because the U. S. transport planes requested by I.R.O. had been diverted to the Far East after the outbreak of the Korean War.[13]

After a few years the processing cooperative folded and the building reverted to its previous function as the Town garage and maintenance building. Leisure, rather than lima beans, seemed destined to be the Island's principal business. Meanwhile the former Dering Harbor Golf Club was reopened after a decade of disuse, under the new name, Gardiner's Bay Country Club. Now, thanks to the vigorous enterprise of the local Lions Club, golf would no longer be a pastime peculiar to the summer people.

That year—1952—marks the Island's tercentenary, at least from the white man's perspective, and the whole population joined in celebrating the occasion. The old windmill was returned to working order. Nathaniel Sylvester's arrival in Dering Harbor was vividly reenacted by a large cast, including Andrew Fiske, the incumbent at Sylvester Manor. Pogaticutt, the Indian chief, stood in proud dignity on Sunset Rock to observe the white man's little boat as it headed into the wide mouth of Second Creek. The subsequent history of the settlement was retraced with the photogenic manor house as one of several "backdrops." A couple of weeks later, an indoor version of the colorful pageant was presented to a very appreciative audience and received the attention of the metropolitan press.

But once again the celebration of a tranquil past was overtaken by the present. As the Korean conflict intensified civil defense activity was resumed. By late 1954 a major exercise had been mounted, based on the supposition that an atom bomb had fallen near Shelter Island and had loosed a wave of heat which set fire to Greenport. Barrels of blazing oil all along the waterfront gave the scene a touch of grim realism. A red alert was sounded and four hundred volunteers were mobilized. Even the Shelter Island ferries were brought into play. A very different kind of "pageant"!

The simulated Korean attack fortunately proved much less destructive than the visit of hurricanes Carol and Edna. In 1953 a severe storm had inundated the business buildings on both sides of Bridge Street, washing forty tons of Piccozzi coal into the harbor. But 1954 was notorious as the year of the hurricanes. Shelter Island, true to its name, escaped the worst. In round figures the damage was summed up as follows: Dering Harbor $2,000, the Heights $2,500, and the rest of the Island $7,650. In the Village, Carol had washed away parts of Shore Road and destroyed many valuable trees. Most deeply regretted was the loss of the great 250-year-old oak that dominated the park behind the Village hall. That handsome specimen had been the pride of the whole community. In the hope of eventually replacing it, one resident, Dr. William Allan, took the initiative in planting a young maple on the same spot.

Dering Harbor's Harbor Master

The Village Board appears to have pursued a steady course, continuing whenever feasible to divest itself of direct responsibility for the public services it had originally acquired or later assumed. By 1955 an agreement had been concluded with the Town's Center Fire Department to provide regular protection in return for the donation of a fire engine and an annual fee. It will be recalled that firefighting equipment for the Village had not been acquired until 1930, years after the Manhanset House burned down. After the sale of the power plant, the fire engine became the chief paladin of political independence. Perhaps in some degree to counteract this new loss, it was decided to float a $17,000 bond issue, making possible the erection of a handsome new water tank atop the highest hill.

Other measures characteristic of the quiet period included lopping ten feet from the top of the old smokestack in 1956, and the cancellation of all unpaid light, water and trash collection bills in 1957. Then in 1958, in addition to repairing some chairs in the Hall and the ceiling in the clerk's office, the Board asked the Town to provide police service for the Village—and Allan Towl was appointed Harbor Master. There is nothing in the records to indicate whether the Village had ever enjoyed regular police protection, although it will be recalled that the redoubtable Professor Poor had once served as deputy sheriff. Back in the days of the Manhanset House, its night watchman had been sworn in by the sheriff as a peace officer.[14] In any event, aside from the matter of water supply and trash collection, the Village was integrating its affairs more and more closely with those of the growing Town.

In general, summer visitors and year-round residents benefited from the steady improvement of the Island's amenities, both public and private. For one thing, the ferry terminal in Greenport was moved in 1958 from the foot of congested Main Street to a new slip next to the Long Island Railroad station. The following year the old waiting room, veteran of many storms including hurricane Donna, was replaced on the Shelter Island side; a couple of years later a new boat, the *Shelter Island*, was added to the fleet.

For another thing, a weekly paper, the *Shelter Island Reporter*, made its tentative appearance, and gradually acquired a footing in the community. Between 1950 and 1960 the Island's population grew from 1,144 to 1,281 residents—a quite respectable increment—and the tide of seasonal visitors was mounting. The question of linking the North and South Forks by a pair of bridges was again raised, and there was also a very serious proposal by the county for a major airport in the Mashomack Forest; but neither project survived the planning stage.

During this relatively quiet decade the composition of Dering Harbor's cottage-owning populace did not change nearly so much as in the decades immediately before and after it. Only two of the large houses changed hands, both of which were substantially improved by their new owners. The one-time country club, now known as Granada, was purchased by Arthur Roth, at that time president of Franklin National Bank, who laid out a long-range program of renovation. The old Schickel house—aptly dubbed Mostly Hall by its new owner, Mrs. Rachel Carpenter—was gradually integrated with three others of the five Germantown properties into one well-manicured unit. For a few years she served as trustee of the Village. The effect of her generous gifts and investments has been felt throughout the Island.

Several other properties were handed down to widows or to the next generation in the same family. Edmund and Alfred Poor, for instance, inherited the properties of their parents, who died within two years of each other. Also, two sons and a daughter who for twenty-five years had shared the property of the first Samuel Hird eventually divided the estate, whereby one son, Henry, received the house in 1950 and the other son, S. Ainsworth, was able to buy the neighboring Forrest Towl cottage a couple of years later. Two other prominent villagers, Gordon Edwards and James Heatherton, left cottages to their widows. Obviously, none of these real estate transactions occasioned major dislocations in the community, though they signaled the end of an era that is appropriately designated that of Charles Lane Poor.

The only effort at further development during this time, in the sense of new construction, occured (very quietly) in the far corner of the Village near Dinah's Rock. Dr. John Frosina, a physician from Douglaston, New York, who had opened an office in the Heights around 1954, acquired two of the bungalows in Land's End from Mr. Hench—namely, the former cook's bungalow and the cottage that had been assembled from, shall we say, miscellaneous dependencies of the Land's End estate. In the next two years the new owner sold them both,[15] then built himself a little house near the waterfront on the remaining land. This latter action appears to have been taken despite an understanding at the time of purchase that no new structure would be erected. In reply to questions, Dr. Frosina pointed out—quite correctly—that he had applied for and received the requisite building permit. The circumstances invite speculation as to whether such a misunderstanding could have occurred while Professor Poor was still living.

Soon thereafter the Board of Trustees for the first time required a fee to be paid in connection with the submission of plans for both building and razing. In 1958 the amount—which today begins at $100—was modestly set at $10.

Chapter X

THE ENVIRONMENTAL FUTURE
1960-1974

THE 1960s will probably go down in American history books as a time of turbulence indelibly associated with the Vietnam War, the civil rights movement and student unrest. None of these traumatic developments struck the sheltered isle with hurricane force, yet it is notable that by 1973 the population of the little Village had undergone an almost complete turnover. More than two-thirds of its cottages—twenty-three to be exact—changed hands at least once. Four of them changed hands twice. All told, there were twenty-seven changes of title among the thirty houses! Notwithstanding the fact that a few of these changes represented nothing more than a transfer of ownership to a younger generation within the same family, it could hardly be doubted that Dering Harbor, along with thousands of other American neighborhoods, had been heavily hit by that common affliction of the 1960s, chronic mobility.

In 1959 a new mayor brought highly professional qualifications from one of the world's biggest municipalities to one of the smallest. George Roy Genung had been Director of Management of the New York City Housing Authority for twenty-three years, including close association with Mayor Fiorello (Little Flower) LaGuardia. At the end of World War II the Genungs had rescued one of the original gingerbread houses from dilapidation, carefully restoring it to nearly mint condition. This cottage also enjoys the unique distinction of occupying a 60-by-100-foot lot as laid out by the original planners of Shelter Island Park. Mayor Genung presided over the affairs of the Village for twelve rather tense years.

In a time of exploding population, the Village was experiencing change without growth. The number of cottages remained almost constant at thirty— a net increase of barely half a dozen residences since the turn of the century, including two beautiful new ones built within the last few years. These recent additions—the first major construction in three decades—preempted the last available shorefront acreage, except for the site once occupied by the main unit of the Manhanset House.[1] But there was still plenty of space for another thirty homes in Dering Harbor's wooded hinterland.

Elsewhere on the Island, houses were springing up like mushrooms. Because of an increasing demand for electric power and for better service, the

Shelter Island Lighting Company, which had absorbed the Dering Harbor plant, was in turn swallowed up by the Long Island Lighting Company. Using Lilco figures, the population of "the East End's fastest growing town"—meaning Shelter Island!—jumped from 1,144 in 1950 to 1,312 in 1960, and to 1,702 in 1970. Such statistics were both gratifying and alarming. Gradually, they whetted interest in the idea of a master plan for dealing with the prospect of unrestrained and explosive growth.

During the eight years from 1960 to 1968, as the population index went up by 22 per cent and the ferries seemed to be slowly sinking under heavier traffic, enthusiasm for bridges flared anew. Also a proposal for a major international airport in Mashomack was revived. Nelson Rockefeller, the very personification of civic progress, arrived for a brief visit in 1962, heralded as the first New York governor to set foot on Shelter Island. That particular distinction, however, rests heavily on the assumption that Governor Thomas E. Dewey—like Moses merely viewing the Promised Land—never got off the yacht that brought him into Dering Harbor during an Off-Soundings cruise ten years earlier.

These were the years when first-class postage went up from four cents to five, when the *Shelter Island Reporter* expanded again and a building boom culminated in the construction along Winthrop Road of a fine hotel and restaurant called the Dering Harbor Inn. Built under the aegis of Mrs. Rachel Carpenter, it could be compared in quality and status—if not in size—with the two great hotels the Island had long since lost.

These were also the progressive years in which Shelter Island saw the debut of cable television and direct dialing. At the end of April 1966, the Island's eight telephone operators were duly feted and retired from the switchboard. No longer could the caller simply lift the receiver and utter one or two digits. Usually a name had been enough, and the operators could often advise you that your "party" was not at home! Now it was necessary to dial 749, followed by four numbers: a most cumbersome, impersonal and even time-consuming procedure. The digits making up each call number were now considerably larger than the entire resident population of the Town.

Moreover, Caleb Dawson's meat market, which had been a landmark family business in the Heights since 1878, closed its doors after ninety years of first-class service. Progress?

Unlike the changing Town, the Village still retained all the somnolent character of a *summer* resort. Whereas the rest of Shelter Island now consisted of "first" and "second" homes in roughly equal proportions, Dering Harbor continued to be overwhelmingly a community of the latter. Of course, the distinction between summer and winter homes was rapidly dwindling as the second-home owners concentrated on making their vacation weeks and weekends more comfortable. Electric refrigerators had long since replaced iceboxes, just as electric washing machines had replaced those "stationary tubs" of which the early families had been so proud. Bottle gas had superseded coal, except on occasional chilly evenings when coal burned in open grates framed by marble mantel pieces. Even the once-unplastered cottages had been at least partly plastered or otherwise insulated against spells of unseasonal weather. Servants were, for the most part, rapidly disappearing. Radio and television drastically reduced the number of expeditions to the Greenport Theater, where the pervasive odor of popcorn was in striking contrast to the salt air and whiffs of diesel oil on the open ferry.

The upgrading of properties was particularly apparent in the transformation of one of the old stables. In 1959 Burns Jenkins, "a nationally famed political cartoonist" for the *New York World* and subsequently for Hearst's *American*,[2] bought a carriage house from the Belle Schwarzmann estate and completely rebuilt it.[3] This was the building put up sixty-five years before by the Reverend Dr. Moore for his seven horses, after he acquired the Roosevelt cottage near Locust Point.[4] By the time Jenkins had finished redoing it, every indication of its previous function as a stable had been thoroughly erased.

Thanks to the constantly improving technology of good housekeeping, not to mention the Long Island Expressway, the ritual associated with the opening and closing of cottages was fast becoming no more than locking up one house and unlocking another. Many owners stretched the summer season to include spring and fall. Custom and circumstance no longer combined to require families, as in an earlier generation, to patronize the boarding houses— Belle Crest, Shelter Island House, etc.—when they came for an off-season weekend. Less attention was given to shrouding all the furniture in dust covers, rolling up the rugs and fastening the shutters over all the windows. Of course, pipes still had to be drained in deep winter, unless the thermostat was simply turned low from weekend to weekend.

Split-Level Loyalties

A new pattern of living was emerging on the Island that might be described as "semi-permanent residence," a kind of split-level allegiance to two communities. Influenced no doubt by the restless mobility of the whole nation, some people commuted off-island to work while others commuted on-island to rest. Inevitably the gap between summer visitors and permanent residents began to close. As the weekenders appeared ever more frequently, an incipient trend in the direction of year-round residence became evident even in Dering Harbor.

A rather careful demographic survey, completed by the Village in January 1974 in preparation for its own master plan, brought the changing pattern clearly into focus. In the decade of 1963-73 the number of cottages occupied by owners rather than tenants rose from twenty to twenty-eight. In other words, rental properties dropped from eight to two, an almost total reversal of the situation prevailing in the pre-Village era and up through the depression years, when the large majority of the cottages could be rented. During the same decade the number of winterized houses rose from twelve to twenty-one and those suited to "summer use only" dropped from ten to two.

The changing concept of vacation was, of course, largely responsible for this. Instead of a "lump sum" holiday of perhaps three or four weeks in July and August, there was a growing tendency—especially on the part of those with freedom to arrange their own working schedules—to prefer long weekends, which by adroit manipulation could be stretched to provide innumerable mini-vacations throughout the year. For a growing percentage of mobile and affluent Americans, shuttling between two homes was standard operating procedure. The weekend was evolving into a new life style. The relatively modest price of this new way of life was paid—not without grumbling protest—by spending extra hours in traffic tieups on crowded highways.

Transfer of legal residence to the Village and the Island was on the upswing again. Mayor Poor had been a strong advocate of local registration and had prevailed on several of the earlier cottage owners to follow his example. By 1963, however, the number of registered voters had dwindled to no more than one or two households. Ten years later it had risen to exactly one-half! The process of re-identification was taking effect.

Legal residence, of course, must not be construed as the equivalent of unbroken year-round residence—which, so far as Dering Harbor was concerned, continued to be the rare exception rather than the rule. Only a couple of owners were actually spending all but the darkest and coldest weeks of the year in their comfortable cottages before fleeing south in search of a sunnier spot. Until the 1950s—that is, for at least eighty years—the only truly year-round resident of Locust Point was the fulltime caretaker who made his home in the superintendent's cottage. News articles about the "deserted village" took pleasure in dwelling upon this unusual feature, pointing out that in 1951, for instance, there was a permanent population of only four persons—namely the Barice Nevéis and their two small children. The distinction of becoming the first bona fide year-round owner-resident seems to belong to Mrs. Rachel Carpenter of Mostly Hall, who for a number of years went to Florida in a private railway car. Considerably later, Lieutenant Colonel and Mrs. John Reeve settled into their Land's End bungalow on a year-round basis.

As a result of these changing patterns, along with many other factors, 1970 inaugurated not simply a new decade but a new era, inside as well as outside the Village. By now environmental concerns had come to be regarded as planetary problems rather than a matter of inhaling good country air in the summer. Monumemtal questions boiled up out of the turbulence of the previous decade. Where is technological progress taking us? What is happening to us and to the world around us? On a national level, the question of human rights was overtaken by the question of human existence. On a global level, the growing need for food and shelter became a gnawing anxiety as to whether the earth's primary resources— namely arable land, clean air and fresh water— would be adequate for tomorrow. So far as Long Island was concerned, the specific issues were the conservation of dwindling farmland, protection of remaining wetlands, stricter zoning, the proposal for a new Peconic county, offshore oil drilling and, above all, the desirability of more long-range planning.

Suffolk County—the largest farm county in New York State—had long been noted for its big potato harvests. Vast open fields punctuated by cavernous storage sheds characterized the refreshingly rural approaches to the Shelter Island ferries. But in the short space of ten years the number of potato farms had dropped from six hundred to fewer than two hundred.[5] Consequently New York State, which had stood sixth in potato production in the nation, was no longer among the first ten. Meanwhile Suffolk County's population more than doubled and land values soared, taking taxes with them. Farms engaged in diversified agriculture-cauliflower, cabbage, corn, strawberries, dairy products— declined from 1,258 to 700 in the same period. Farmers were selling out to developers. The ultimate effect of this on Long Island's economy and its vacation industry was obvious to the county executive, John V. N. Klein, who initiated a bold policy of protecting agriculture by purchasing "development rights" from the farmer to encourage continued cultivation. In other words, such acreages would be permanently removed from the real estate developers' market. This $45-million program began with the purchase of the first 68 acres in the summer of 1974.

Mayor Wilcox's Master Plan

While Suffolk County—along with the rest of the nation—probed the full meaning of that newly-popular word ecology, the Village was again in the process of changing guard. At the regular 1970 election Thomas R. Wilcox,[6] a vice president of the First National City Bank in New York, received a majority of the seventeen votes cast and succeeded George Roy Genung as mayor. Renouncing the nominal stipend of $400 per year, he applied his considerable drive to Village affairs. The new mayor had moved to Dering Harbor only six years before, but he and his wife had been intimately acquainted with the Island for many years. On Monday mornings, as a general rule, he would walk down Yoco Road from his house to the beach where a small seaplane taxied up to carry him to Manhattan—and to bring him back on Friday for a weekend of attention to local matters.

Responsibility for major aspects of Village business was now parceled out among the various trustees, more or less according to the budgetary divisions. These included buildings and grounds, utilities, finance and also a portfolio on public relations. One of the first decisions of the new administration was to abolish separate billing for water use and trash collection; charges for these services were absorbed in the general budget. As various other issues came under systematic scrutiny that first summer, a revised list of ordinances, or local laws, was drawn up. Revision is hardly an accurate term. The three or four ordinances previously adopted over a period of fifty-odd years seem to have been forgotten. By contrast, the Wilcox administration enacted eleven new "local laws" in its first two years, causing the *Shelter Island Reporter* to refer to a "deluge" of restrictions—against letting dogs run loose, littering, soliciting, beach buggying, overboard dumping and anchoring within 400 feet of the shoreline.[1]

As a matter of fact, the new Board was interested in much more than mere legislative nitpicking. One of the very first Village laws dealt with the crucial question of zoning. It established—not without controversy—a three-acre minimum for the construction of cottages on land not yet subdivided for building purposes. Most of the other above-mentioned ordinances were adopted, after scrutiny of the Town's laws, simply in order to establish a legal basis for action against public nuisances as circumstances might require.

Out of these legislative discussions and piecemeal enactments, two principal objectives soon emerged. The first was a thorough overhaul of the public property and premises. The "maintenance area," so-called, was an unsightly clutter of deteriorating buildings surrounded by undergrowth, fortunately hidden from passers-by at the upper end of Yoco Road. After the fire of 1896, many important but preferably invisible hotel services had been banished to this spot. Most of these, such as the barns, the stables, the ice house and the old water tank, had been dismantled. Others, such as the power station and superintendent's house, had ceased to serve their original purpose.

A major reclamation effort was directed by trustee Ian Brownlie, whose portfolio was grounds and buildings, ably seconded by Clifton Phalen, whose assignment was utilities. First, the decrepit and and disused house (onetime laundry) was razed following a futile effort to sell it. Next the tall smokestack, which had been moved to its present location after the 1896 fire and was almost the last surviving relic of the very first hotel, was brought low and successfully offered for sale at five cents per brick. The old power station was completely transformed into a spacious, well-lighted maintenance center. Meanwhile tangled thickets that concealed the rusting skeletons of an automobile and other machinery were cleared away and grass was planted. The result: a back yard to vie with the attractive front yard of the Village.

Actually the front yard, or at least the Village hall, needed some attention also. The two wings of the building containing the clerk's office and the board room urgently required both repair and redecorating. One thing led to another. Mayor Wilcox presented a full complement of handsome furniture for both the board room and the larger hail-whereupon the previous furnishings that had first been borrowed, then purchased, from Mayor Poor were sold, except for his splendid rolltop desk, which was handsomely refinished. Learning that further renovation was beyond the Village budget, Mrs. Florence McCormick, who had recently acquired the Hench house, quietly underwrote both the redecoration of the large hall and the exterior painting. To celebrate the completion of all this work, the trustees, at their own expense, invited the Village to an open house in June 1972, at which time a mayor's flag, bearing the seal of the Village, was presented to Mr. Wilcox.

In many ways Dering Harbor was becoming a closely knit community again. This was owing, in part, to the fact that more people were spending more time on the Island.[8] There was a revived sense of participation in a common enterprise. In connection with the so-called "deluge" of ordinances, for example, it was noted that for the first time in a quarter century public hearings were being held on non-budgetary as well as budgetary matters. In fact, only three such public hearings had ever before been conducted.[9]

The second principal objective of the Wilcox administration—much more far-reaching than repair and renovation of public property—was a master plan for the future development of the Village. It grew out of the recognition that change and growth were inevitable and not necessarily undesirable. The aim of the long-range planning was to pinpoint some future goals and begin working toward them according to a generally acceptable timetable. This was in no sense an isolated or selfish concern, but one that was belatedly engaging the attention of hundreds of communities alarmed by a variety of critical problems: urban decay, polluted air, dying lakes, ravaged beachfronts, strip mining and endangered wildlife, to mention only a few.

Importance of Wetlands and Water

One of the main issues on Shelter Island was the preservation of miles of shoreline, especially the tidal marshes which were all too often regarded as useless or worthless until they were drained and filled for residential or industrial purposes. Under the motto "Wetlands are not Wastelands," a new ordinance to protect these areas was adopted by the Town in 1972. The Village expressed its unqualified approval and support of this measure. Full credit was given to an aroused citizenry. "Mounting public pressure over the past two years coupled with a petition signed by 1529 residents and presented to the Town Board in August gave impetus to the proposal and passage of the ordinance."[10]

The donation by public-spirited summer residents of four pieces of Shelter Island woodland and wetland totaling some twenty-five acres reinforced these protective measures in a very tangible way. The recipient and trustee of these precious tracts is The Nature Conservancy, a national agency dedicated to the preservation of environmentally significant areas.

To the surprise of many people, the most crucial factor in any appraisal of future possibilities was the problem not of adequate land but of adequate water. It had been assumed that an almost unlimited supply of fresh water lay untapped below the level of existing wells on Shelter Island. Test borings, however, disclosed that this was not a fact. On the contrary, extreme care would have to be exercised to prevent salt-water intrusion from contaminating the depleted reservoirs of sweet water. Therefore the prospective increase in population would have to be geared primarily to available water rather than to available land. It was believed that Shelter Island represented one of the first instances in which the supply of fresh water was taken as the main determinant in long-range planning.

The Village of Dering Harbor itself was not confronted by any immediate crisis, but the makings of one were present. Over half of its two hundred wooded acres remained "unimproved" and higher taxes were forcing the owners of large holdings to think seriously of subdividing. More homes would of course require more water. Two preliminary lines of action were foreseen by the Trustees in their effort to cope with these eventualities: first, a zoning ordinance, already mentioned which established a minimum of three acres for all new building lots in the interior; secondly, a plan for gradually extending Village ownership of the area around the water tower and existing wells, for the dual purpose of protecting the present wells and of digging new ones as needed. The first step was taken in 1974 when the trustees bought the small plot immediately adjacent to the water tower—none other than the lot on which the Manhanset Chapel had been built in 1890.

The larger task of preparing a comprehensive plan still lay ahead. The zoning ordinance in itself, aside from setting a three-acre minimum, did little or nothing to suggest optimum development of the wooded areas. Consultants from the Suffolk County Department of Planning were called in to make a careful study of all factors and submit their recommendations. In July 1974 a preliminary report was submitted to the Village at an informational meeting. Proceeding on the basis of the existing three-acre restriction, the consultants suggested alternative proposals whereby about thirty new homes could be built, in ways calculated to preserve the most attractive features of the present Village.

Meanwhile, on January 1, 1974, Deputy Mayor Brownlie became acting mayor and a few months later succeeded to the office resigned by Mayor Wilcox when he moved to California as president of the Crocker National Bank—without, however, relinquishing either his Dering Harbor cottage or the old hotel acreage, which had recently been acquired as the site for a new summer home. The latter plans were merely postponed.

The seventh mayor—a realtor from New York City—had become a resident of the Village several years earlier upon purchasing the fine house built in 1915 by Dering Harbor's second mayor, Charles Lane Poor. That property, after nearly sixty years of steady use, inevitably needed a certain amount of refurbishing, to which the Brownlies wholeheartedly applied themselves. The interior of the graceful structure was thoroughly modernized and winterized; outside, the grounds were restored to what approached, or even surpassed, the carefully tended, parklike appearance of the Manhanset grove in its famed heyday.

Manhanset House Remembered

Exactly one hundred years had rolled by since the once-famous hotel first opened its doors on the bluff above Greenport Channel, and there was unanimous agreement that the anniversary should not pass unnoticed. Two events were planned—a community picnic and a historical display.

The "old fashioned Centennial Picknick" was held on August 3, 1974, on the tree-shaded grounds of the former Manhanset House, which had been a popular spot for Island outings long before the hotel was built. The weather that afternoon—warm sun and a light breeze—could not have been better. By 5 P.M. approximately one hundred Villagers and their friends had found places on the grass for their blankets and chairs. Mr. and Mrs. Genung took seriously the invitation to come "as you were" by arriving in authentic nineteenth century dress. Later Mr. Genung received a plaque in appreciation of his services as mayor, and Mrs. Helen Loper received similar recognition for her many years of service as Village clerk.

Otherwise the picnic was just a feast of food and fun. Some joined in the games—potato-sack races, three-legged races, etc.—and some joined in song to the accompaniment of an accordion. Others just stood around and talked. All ate. There were—for the record—steamed clams to start with, then chicken (Kentucky fried), a variety of homemade salads, lots of layer cake and chilled watermelon. And two main beverages: lemonade and beer.

The other event, the Centennial Exhibit, took place in the Village Hall, where a series of seven large canary-yellow panels had been arranged in roughly chronological order. Many large photographs and other souvenirs—arranged and embellished by Carl and Sue Gustafson—conveyed visual impressions of the great hotel and its cottages, the subsequent country club and the development of the Village.

But the display, which attracted well over two hundred visitors in the course of ten days, was not merely nostalgic. The final panel pointed toward the smaller Trustees' Room, in which the Master Plan proposals were graphically displayed for further study. The message was clear: the Village that had "lost a past" when its great summer resort hotel burned down still had a future. Looking backward was—and is—prelude to looking ahead.

Reference Notes

Abbreviations:
LIT The Long Island Traveler
RN The Riverhead News
RW Republican Watchman
SHE Sag Harbor Express
SIR Shelter Island Reporter
SWT Suffolk Weekly Times, also *Suffolk Times*

All deeds mentioned are on file at the Suffolk County Center in Riverhead.
Village documents, such as minutes, official correspondence, and the historical essay of Mayor Poor, are in the Village archives, except for some
Poor files in the possession of Mayor Ian Brownlie.

Chapter I
1. Harold C. Schonberg, *The New York Times*, Sept. 12, 1971.
2. Ralph G. Duvall, *History of Shelter Island*, privately published, 1952, p. 190.

Chapter II
1. *LIT*, Oct. 3, 1872.
2. *RW*, Sept. 5, 1874.
3. From articles reprinted in i?W, Aug. 15 and 22, 1874.
4. *SWT*, Feb. 24, 1883.
5. *LIT*, Aug. 6, 1874.
6. Reprinted in *RW*, Aug. 22, 1874.
7. From *Appleton's Journal*, 1870; quoted in *Greenport, Yesterday and Today* by Elsie Knapp Corwin, p. 55.
8. Reprinted in 7?W, Aug. 1,1874.
9. *RW*, Sept. 5, 1874.
10. *Springfield Republican* (Mass.), July 30, 1873.
11. *Greenport, Yesterday and Today* by Elsie K. Corwin.
12. Now owned by the Shelter Island Historical Society.
13. *SWT*, Aug. 19, 1876.
14. *RW*, Aug. 16,1873.

15. *RW*, Aug. 15, 1874.
16. *SWT*, July 16, 1926.
17. Ralph G. Duvall, *History of Shelter Island*, p. 181.
18. *SWT*, Aug. 19, 1876.
19. *SWT*, Aug. 19, 1876.
20. *Brooklyn Eagle*, Aug. 6, 1874.
21. *SWT*, Aug. 25, 1877.
22. Cf. *SIR*, April-June 1960, an informative series of weekly articles by May Piccozzi, "When Is A Ferry?"
23. Promotional flyer, 1873.
24. *SWT*, March 24, 1877.
25. It was on this road that a barrier stood about where the Village boundary line now runs. Cf. May Piccozzi, *SIR*, April 23, 1960.
26. *SWT*, June 15, 1878.
27. *Brooklyn Eagle*, July 31, 1875.
28. Four concrete bases and an equal number of old locust posts that once supported this pavilion were removed in 1974, approximately a century later.
29. *RW*, Aug. 15,1874.
30. *SWT*, October 1880.
31. *Union Argus*, Aug. 8, 1878.

Chapter III
1. Now owned by Dr. Wm. B. Allan, Roy Genung and Walter Glaws.
2. The kitchen annexes may have been added in 1889, when the Woodand Headley cottages—now owned by Genung and Allan—were"enlarged." Cf. *UT*, March 29, 1889.
3. Cf. Suffolk Co. Deeds, Motley-Pond to Headley, Liber 377, p. 427, Dec. 18, 1891.
4. *SWT*, Nov. 3, 1883.
5. Deeds, Liber 285, p. 583, Lot #17.
6. Deeds, Liber 286, p. 75; also *SWT*, Nov. 15, 1884.
7. Now Westgate (Vernon O'Rourke).
8. Now Walter Glaws.
9. *SWT*, Aug. 18, 1877.
10. *SWT*, July 24, 1886.
11. C. F. Bateman survey of 1872, registered with Suffolk Co.
12. *SWT*, Feb. 24, 1883, written by regular contributor from Shelter Island.
13. *SWT*, May 26, 1883.
14. Now owned by Stewart W. Herman.
15. The 1884 Bateman cottage, razed 1923, stood where Arnott White is now. Cartwright's, now Morgan Ames, was relocated and completely remodeled in 1979. Prof. Poor dates both houses circa 1880, which is too early.

16. Cf. *SWT*, Jan. 29, 1887. These cottages are now owned by J. E.Blackburn, Mrs. Gordon Edwards and Mathias Komor, although the last-mentioned was extensively transformed in 1932 and named Eastgate. Prof. Poor dates all three circa 1880, but the news item seems more reliable.

17. *LIT*, Dec. 20, 1889, and Jan. 31, 1890. The Woodhouse cottage is now occupied by Mrs. Marie Bay lis.

18. Probably Harold Weaver.

19. Deeds. Shelter Island Park to Mrs. Helen Motley. Liber 266, p. 375, July 20, 1882.

20. The original Manhanset stable was an exception and stood, with the water tower, in the now well-wooded area directly across from the present Village hall.

21. Now Peacock-Adams, Mrs. Henry Kohl and Frederick Bruenner respectively. Only Peacock-Adams retains the large stable doors.

22. *LIT* June 11, 1886.

23. *SWT*, July 12, 1884.

24. *SWT*, Sept. 13, 1884.

25. *LIT*, July 9, 1886.

26. *LIT*, July 16, 1886.

27. *SWT*, May 26, 1883.

28. Manhanset House brochure of 1886.

29. *SWT*, June 21 and July 21, 1884.

30. *SWT*, Feb. 23, 1884.

31. Many years later Dr. Fowler's son gave these mementos to Dr. Wm. B. Allan, who donated them to the Village archives.

32. *SWT*, Aug. 16, 1884.

33. *SWT*, Aug. 25, 1883.

34. *SWT*, Oct. 4, 1884.

35. *SWT*, Oct. 6, 1883.

36. *SWT*, Sept. 10, 1887.

37. *LIT*, July 25, 1890, quoting the *Brooklyn Eagle*.

Chapter IV

1. *SWT*, March 5, 1887.

2. *SWT*, Sept. 15, 1900.

3. *LIT*, Aug. 24, 1888.

4. Deeds, Liber 245, p. 15.

5. *LIT*, May 2, 1890.

6. *LIT*, Feb. 27, 1891.

7. The Schickel house, now Mrs. Carpenter's Mostly Hall, remains relatively unchanged. A swimming pool occupies the approximate site of the Pickhardt house razed in 1959; its garage still stands nearby. The Kuttroff cottage, now Mrs. McCormick, was moved back and

extensively remodeled and faced with brick in 1937. Mrs. Schwarzmann razed the Lidgerwood house in 1945 and converted its basement into a toolhouse. Mrs. Carpenter razed the Schwarzmann cottage in 1963.

8. This was the house on Patchogue built by Motley and Pond in 1886, occupying the north end of what is now the Dr. George Read lot.

9. *SWT*, Aug. 2, and Sept. 6, 1884.

10. Personal recollection of Alfred Easton Poor in 1973.

11. The Anthony house, after frequent remodeling, became the present Eastgate.

12. This house was erected on the south end of the now Read lot at the corner of Shore Road and Gardiner Way. It burned down in 1911 after barely a decade of use.

13. *LIT*, Sept. 2, 1892.

14. *SWT*, Oct. 6, 1883.

15. Moore had bought the cottage now occupied by Mrs. Bay lis after the death of Grace Roosevelt; the stable is the present Mrs. Jane Kohl cottage. For a full account of the stable fire and reconstruction see *LIT*, March 29 and Apr. 12, 1895.

16. *LIT*, Nov. 15 and Feb. 28, 1896.

17. Manhanset House promotional booklet of 1908. The old clubhouse is now Hine off Cobbett Lane.

18. *SHE*, March 2, 1950.

19. Including Eastgate, Westgate and Herman.

20. *LIT*, Oct. 21,1896.

21. This smokestack, long unused, was finally demolished in 1972 and its bricks sold for five cents each.

22. Cf. Poor's historical essay of 1933.

23. *RN*, May 30, 1903.

24. *LIT*, June 4, 1897, quoting A*T. Y. Tribune*, which consistently seemed to favor Prospect House.

25. Duvall, *History of Shelter Island, p.* 212.

26. Now Mrs. Henrietta Roig.

27. Subsequent owner, J. W. Heatherton, mistakenly believed that the house was built in 1897.

28. *Mrs. Fiske and the American Theatre* by Archie Binns, New York: Crown Publishers, 1955. A letter addressed to the author in 1973 elicited a reply from his daughter stating that her father had died and all his notes were lost or stolen.

29. *SWT*, Aug. 5, 1899.

30. *LIT*, Oct. 6,1893.

31. *LIT* July 12, 1895.

32. *SWT*, May 19, 1900.

33. *RN*, July 20, 1901.

34. *LIT*, June 11,1886.

35. *SWT*, July 14,1900.
36. *RN*, July 20, 1901.
37. An 1898 reprint in *SIR*, March 28, 1964. The same scholarly Dr. J. E. Mallmann wrote an early history of Shelter Island up to 1812.

Chapter V

1. *RN, Aug.* 17, 1901.
2. *RN*, Oct. 27 and Nov. 10, 1903.
3. *SWT*, Sept. 22, 1900.
4. Poor's historical essay, 1933.
5. *SIR*, June 26, 1965.
6. Now Ames.
7. All quotes from *Bishop of Broadway: David Belasco* by Craig Timberlake,
8. *SWT*, Sept. 28, 1907.
9. Deeds, Liber 684, p. 251, Apr. 30, 1909; also Liber 774, p. 237, June 1, 1911, for inventory of buildings and other details.
10. Identifiable today, since street numbers still mean very little, as Genung, Herman, Weaver, Blackburn and Komor: Oaklawn is still unknown. Of course the cottage names often changed with the owner and/or a new coat of paint. Homecrest later became Eastgate, and Kenwood became Red Cottage.
11. Poor's historical essay, 1933.
12. Now Herman.
13. *SWT*, Feb. 4, 1911.
14. *SWT*, Apr. 22, 1911.
15. *SWT*, May 20, 1911.
16. *SIR*, Nov. 28, 1970.
17. The great mathematician, incidentally, once took a cottage at Nassau Point on the North Fork and thereafter maintained contact with friends around Southold for many years. *SWT*, Apr. 28, 1938.
18. Larchmont Yacht Club Yearbook, 1904.
19. Now Glaws.

Chapter VI

1. Now Granada's main building owned by Arthur Roth.
2. *SWT*, Aug. 23, 1935.
3. Alfred Easton Poor, in a 1973 conversation with the author, distinctly recalled relatives and friends of his family staying in this Annex of the Manhanset House when it was located between the present Village hall and Eastgate.
4. Now Granada's annex.
5. Now Allan.
6. *SWT*, Apr. 18, 1914. Now Peter Holnback; Mrs. Holnback is Samuel Hird's granddaughter.

7. Now Blackburn.
8. SWT, June 8, 1923.
9. Oct. 15, 1915.
10. Known as the Percy cottage, it had most recently contained hotel offices and was purchased by Benjamin Atha a year or so before for $3,000. Evidently he transferred it to the Village at less than cost. See next chapter for further details.
11. The *Brooklyn Eagle* rhapsodized over "lucky Shelter Island" the "only town in the county" with no one in the almshouse or the children's home and therefore unencumbered by charges at those county institutions. *SWT*, Jan. 17, 1914.
12. Now Ian Brownlie.
13. Now Samuel Hird, grandson of the first Samuel.
14. Now Dr. George Read.
15. The Red Cottage, once known as Kenwood, is now Weaver. The new house is now Thos. R. Wilcox.
16. SWT, Oct. 5, 1917.
17. Straus letter of Oct. 1, 1918, in the Poor archives.
18. Poor to Straus, Jan. 31, 1919 in the Poor archives.
19. Owner of the Bateman cottage, now White.
20. In a letter dated Apr. 7, 1974, Mr. Henry E. Hird, son of Samuel, states, "It was he [i.e., the father] that helped to organize the golf club and put $8,000 into the project for which, when the club folded up, he received eighty acres of woodland for his investment."

Chapter VII
1. Cf. Poor's historical essay, 1933.
2. Now White and Allan, respectively.
3. Cf. Poor's historical essay, 1933.
4. A few years later, in 1927, the last "king of the Montauks," Sam Pharoah, was found frozen to death on the South Fork near Three Mile Harbor. He was a direct descendant of Wyandanch, the brother of Yoco.
5. LIT, Aug. 16, 1895.
6. SWT, March 1924.
7. The house had actually been sold in 1919 to Thos. Burns, a well-known island builder and contractor who offered it for summer rental, but the name Atha evidently clung to it.
8. SWT July 30, 1926.
9. SWT, July 9, 1926.
10. SWT, Feb. 5, 1926.
11. As noted above, this is now Granada, owned by Roth.
12. Now Wilcox and Read, respectively.
13. Now Mrs. Henrietta Roig.
14. SWT, July 11, 1924.

15. Now White.
16. *SWT* July 18,1924.
17. *SWT* July 8, 1924.
18. *SWT*, Aug. 26, 1927.

Chapter VIII

1. Village Minutes, July 7 and Aug. 9, 1930.
2. Mayor Putnam to Attorney Tasker in 1918.
3. This staff house was razed in the early 1970s.
4. Village Minutes, Mar. 8, 1928.
5. Total actual cost, according to Mayor Poor in 1932, was $15,615.35.
6. Village Minutes, June 1, 1931.
7. Mrs. Loper, at present writing, continues to function as Village clerk, with a remarkably fine record of loyal and effective service ever since 1936.
8. Minutes, Sept. 19, 1931. Subsequently, W. P. Pickhardt bid in the Yoco landing, now Wilcox beach. The Dering Lane footage was bought, rather reluctantly, by Prudden and is now White shorefront.
9. Now Read.
10. Feb. 24, 1938.
11. *SWT* 1930.
12. *SWT*, Sept. 25, 1931; now Allan.
13. *SWT*, Dec. 4, 1931.
14. *SWT*, Jan. 25, 1935.
15. Now Allan.
16. Now Wilcox.
17. Poor archives, Nov. 11, 1929.
18. Now McCormick. Despite the sale of the Kuttroff house, the family name did not become extinct in the Village for another thirty years. Bachelor son, Edwin, first rented and later bought the "Piel Cottage," now Baylis, and in his later years continued to row across the harbor daily to fetch his mail from the Heights post office.
19. *SWT*, June 21 and Nov. 8, 1935; also *SIR*, June 11, 1960.

Chapter IX

1. Commodore John Baylis, who later spent many summer weekends in the Village, was then port captain and second in command of the N. Y. District Coast Guard; he was personally involved in quashing this melodramatic "invasion."
2. *SWT*, *July* 17, 1941.
3. *SWT*, Dec. 18, 1941.
4. *SWT*, Oct. 14, 1943.
5. *SWT*, Sept. 30, 1943; Sept. 22, 1944.
6. *SWT*, Sept. 25, 1941.
7. E.g., Allan 1943, Genung 1945, Carpenter 1947, Edwards 1948.

8. Now John Reeve.
9. Now Gustafson.
10. Now Peacock-Adams.
11. Once the hotel's Red Cottage, now Weaver.
12. *SHE*, Oct. 19, 1950.
13. *SHE*, Aug. 24, 1950.
14. *LIT*, July 16, 1886.
15. Namely, to Carl Gustafson and Harvey Wollhiser.

Chapter X

1. The new houses are Clifton Phalen, 1965, and Bridgford Hunt 1971, whose wife, Esther is a granddaughter of Samuel Hird.
2. Jenkins' obituary, *SIR*, March 5, 1966.
3. Now Kohl.
4. Now Baylis. (The Baylis house was bought by Brownlie in 1975)
5. Statistical data from a special dispatch to the *New York Times*, datelined Apr. 6, 1974.
6. Subsequently president of Crocker National Bank, headquartered in San Francisco.
7. *SIR*, Dec. 1971.
8. The Brownlies commuted from New York City almost every weekend; the Phalens, O'Rourkes and Hermans had doubled the number of those who regarded the Village as home base.
9. *SIR*, Dec. 1971.
10. *SIR*, Feb. 5, 1972.

Index

www.ingramcontent.com/pod-product-compliance
Lightning Source LLC
Chambersburg PA
CBHW051718090426
42738CB00010B/1975